W9-AAN-177

CHEESE OBSESSION

recipes
Georgeanne Brennan

photographs
Maren Caruso

weldonowen

Every cheese—and more than three thousand different kinds are made around the world—has its own distinct appearance, texture, aroma, and taste. Those unique qualities owe something to the maker, of course, but also to the land—lush alpine grasses or meadows, valley oaks or pines—on which the animals that produce the milk graze. Cheeses even taste different depending on the season. Many years ago, when I raised goats in Provence, the cheese I made from their milk was richer and creamier in spring when they were feeding on the fresh green grasses and early, tender oak leaves. With the arrival of the hot Mediterranean summer, the grasses dried, and the goats turned to wild thyme and more mature leaves for sustenance. The cheese made during those warm days was tangier and less sweet than its springtime counterpart. Recognizing that difference made me appreciate not only the skill that goes into making cheese, but also the role played by both nature and the farmer who cares for the animals that produce the milk.

Not surprisingly, given my early days as a goatherd and cheese maker, cheese is part of almost every meal I prepare, whether presented as its own course, grated atop a salad, swirled into risotto, melted over vegetables, or served with fruit for dessert. It can also be reason for its own occasion: sampling a special cheese and a good wine with friends is one of life's pleasures, which I savor as often as possible. Indeed, a wedge of great cheese is a wonderful way to bring friends and family together.

Georgeanne Brennan

"Great cheese, like great wine, tastes of the terroir—of the land, the climate, the place where it was produced. Also like wine, cheese is evocative and sensual, drawing all of the senses into a rich gustatory experience."

about cheese

I came to truly understand and appreciate cheese while living in southern France. That rugged landscape still bears visual traces of the Roman occupation, and I was fascinated by the ancient history that links a story of conquest with one of the most beloved of French foods.

history

The Romans, in fact, first brought cheese to France. But cheese spans back even earlier than the Roman Empire, thousands of years before I raised my goats in modern-day Provence. The invention of cheese predates written records; it is believed to have occurred in the Middle East or Central Asia around the same time that sheep were first domesticated. Herders and farmers discovered that curdling and fermenting milk was a useful way to prevent it from spoiling and to stock protein-rich food for the winter months. It was the ancient Greeks who penned the earliest descriptions of cheese making; by Roman times, fashioning cheeses had become a culinary art.

After the fall of Rome, production techniques continued to be refined in Europe. In medieval times, cheeses were routinely crafted on single-family farms and in monasteries. Monks in particular became known for their innovations in the creation and storage of substantial, tasty cheeses, which they routinely consumed during their long meatless fasts. In many areas of Europe, caves were used for aging, and today these natural storage vaults remain essential to the production of certain cheeses, most famously Roquefort.

Centuries later, urbanization brought mass-market food manufacturing and less need for small farms. The Industrial Revolution saw the opening of the first cheese factories, and two world wars ushered in an era in which large-scale production would outstrip natural products. This was particularly true in the United States, home to a vast cattle industry.

artisanal cheese making

Today, the steadily growing artisanal movement in cheese making has brought the cycle full circle, returning us to the farm and the cave. Although handcrafted local cheeses have long been heralded abroad, only in the last decade have small-batch producers appeared in significant numbers in North America. Now in the dairy case, you'll find cheeses from big factories alongside specialty cheeses by regional makers. Some may be farmstead cheeses, produced from the milk of a single farm—not unlike a single-vineyard designation by a winemaker. Connoisseurs swoon over the unique flavor and texture of each of the hundreds of varieties now available. Yet cheese also remains an important staple in the home kitchen, both as an ingredient in countless dishes and as the star on its own plate.

types of cheese

Most cheeses begin the same way: milk is warmed, cultured, and allowed to ferment. Rennet coagulates the milk, and the solids are shaped and aged. Depending on the culture used or the aging technique, the results vary. You can group cheeses by the type of milk used, but it's more useful for cooking to categorize them by the length of aging and their final texture.

fresh

Fresh cheeses are not aged. They are generally made from milk that ferments only briefly before being separated into solid curds and liquid whey. The curds are then drained and pressed into shape or, sometimes, simply wrapped. These cheeses don't keep, so they must be eaten shortly after they are made. Since aging creates flavor, fresh cheeses are among the most mild. They most closely resemble the original character and flavor of the milk from which they were made. For instance, goat's milk imparts a tartness, while cow's milk is mild. Their texture is usually smooth and easily spreadable (except in the cases of ricotta, which is not drained of its whey, and fresh mozzarella, which is a stretched cheese).

examples include Boursin, chèvre, cottage cheese, cream cheese, *crescenza,* farmer cheese, feta, *fromage frais,* fresh mozzarella, mascarpone, *paneer, queso fresco,* and ricotta

natural rind

When fresh cheeses are left to sit in a cellar and dry out, they attract natural molds and yeasts from the air that create a soft, often powdery rind. As the cheese sits and ages—even just for a couple of weeks—this surface becomes thicker and the cheese drier and firmer, often developing a nutty flavor and more pungent aroma and taste. This treatment is used especially with goat cheeses, most famously Crottin de Chavignol.

examples include Banon, Chèvrefeuille, Crottin de Chavignol, Rocamadour, and Selles-sur-Cher

soft-ripened

Soft-ripened cheeses are distinguished by their distinctive rind and ripening process. After the milk is coagulated, these cheeses are placed in molds to shape them and then transferred to straw mats and exposed to particular bacteria (including penicillium) that cause them to develop a soft, powdery white covering known as a "bloomy" rind. These cheeses age from the exterior inward, softening as they mature until their centers are creamy and oozy. They remain moist in the interior, thanks to the moldy coating. When cream is added to the milk content of a soft-ripened cheese, it becomes a "double cream" or "triple cream" cheese, known for its rich and buttery center. These flavorful, unctuous cheeses

Clockwise from bottom Cana de Cabra, Pyramide, Rosso di Langa, Brebirousse D'Argental, Muenster, Brunet, crottin, and pecorino.

are delicious with little embellishment. Served at room temperature, they are easily spreadable, some to the point of being runny.

examples include Brie, Brillat-Savarin, Camembert, Chaource, Explorateur, Humboldt Fog, Montbriac, Neufchâtel, and *pavé d'affinois*

semisoft

This description covers an enormous range of cheeses. Determining whether a cheese should be labeled semisoft is not an exact science. Instead, the judgment is intuitive. Semisoft refers to the moisture, or whey, content of a cheese, and to its resulting degree of softness (a quality that is not necessarily an indicator of higher fat content, as some mistakenly believe). A cheese with relatively more whey is softer; a cheese with less whey is firmer. Semisoft cheeses will keep for a few days longer than fresh ones. In general, the softer the cheese, the shorter the shelf life.

examples include Chaumes, Havarti, Mont d'Or, Morbier, Port-Salut, raclette, Saint-Nectaire, and Teleme (Brie, Camembert, Gorgonzola, and Taleggio may be considered semisoft, but also fall into other categories—soft-ripened, blue, and washed-rind, respectively)

washed-rind

Washed-rind cheeses overlap with the semisoft group, but, as with the soft-ripened cheeses, they distinguish themselves from other cheeses by their particular aging process and distinctive rind. Medieval monks were the first to develop the technique of washing or rinsing cheeses as they aged with water, brine, wine, beer, or brandy, a practice that encourages bacteria to grow. This washing results in orange or russet rinds. Like soft-ripened cheeses, washed-rind cheeses age from the rind inward, and their centers can range from nearly liquid to an almost meaty texture.

These cheeses are known for their pungent aromas, sometimes described as "musty," "gamy," or even "barnyardy." However, their flavors are often much mellower than their aromas, tasting full and delicious.

examples include Époisses de Bourgogne, Limburger, Muenster, Pont-l'Évêque, Reblochon, Saint-Nectaire, and Taleggio

semifirm

The semifirm category, like semisoft, is based on texture. Longer aging and less moisture are the criteria that separate these cheeses from their semisoft cousins, but, again, there is not a clear-cut divide.

Pressing is an important technique for firming cheeses, helping to remove additional whey and create dense, consistent interiors. Curds for semifirm cheeses are generally uncooked, but may be washed or cut before pressing. Washing or rinsing curds will yield a milder flavor, and cutting curds creates a smooth or sometimes rubbery texture; a slice of Colby, for instance, will bend rather than break or crumble. Many semifirm cheeses can last for three to four weeks after opening a package, and even two weeks after slicing.

examples include Cantal, Cheddar, Cheshire, Colby, Edam, Emmentaler, Fontina, Gouda, Gruyère, Comté, Jarlsberg, Lancashire, Mahón, young Manchego, Monterey Jack, low-moisture mozzarella, provolone, *ricotta salata,* and tomme de Savoie

hard

The firmest-textured cheeses are yielded by "cooking" or heating curds until they solidify, and then pressing and aging over a long period of time. While fresh or soft-ripened cheeses go from the dairy to the table in a matter of days or weeks, hard cheeses take at least months and sometimes more

than a year to mature. This lengthy aging dries and hardens the texture, and sharpens the flavor. It also ensures that hard cheeses have a longer shelf life than other cheese types.

examples include Asiago, *grana padano,* dry Jack, aged Manchego, Parmigiano-Reggiano, and various types of pecorino and Romano

blue

Although blue cheeses fall variously under the semisoft, soft-ripened, and semifirm categories, they must also be considered as a group in their own right, due to one characteristic feature that sets them apart from other cheeses: a network of visible blue mold or veins lacing throughout their interior. These veins are what bring blue cheeses their strong flavor, crumbly texture, and striking appearance.

Blue cheeses are created by adding select bacteria to the curds, and by either packing or puncturing the curds loosely. The latter allows air pockets where the mold may grow, ripening the cheese from within. Blue cheese has a distinctive flavor that gains potency with aging. Pungent and salty and sometimes stinky, blues are for some an acquired taste. But those who like them are hard-pressed to pass one up.

examples include bleu d'Auvergne, Cabrales, Cashel blue, Danish blue, Fourme d'Ambert, Gorgonzola *dolce* and *naturale,* Maytag blue, Roquefort, Stilton, and Valdeón

a word on milk

The importance of this primary ingredient to a finished cheese cannot be overstated. Mild cow's milk cheeses are the most common and popular, thanks to the sheer amount of good-quality milk a cow can supply. But goat's and sheep's milk cheeses, as well as mixed-milk varieties, are worth seeking out. Historically, goat's and sheep's milk cheeses were made in rugged, mountainous areas, terrain where raising cattle proved difficult. Goat's milk contains an additional acid that gives cheese made from it a signature tangy, tart flavor. Sheep's milk has a higher butterfat content than goat's milk and yields especially flavorful, distinctively nutty cheeses.

Pasteurization is another factor in defining a finished cheese. Anyone who has had raw-milk Brie or Camembert in France will bemoan how American counterparts pale in comparison. The USDA mandates a sixty-day aging for any cheese made from raw milk, too long for fresh and soft-ripened cheeses, so all cheeses in these categories sold in the United States must be made from pasteurized milk. The trade-off favors public health but sacrifices complexity of flavor.

Clockwise from bottom Point Reyes Original Blue, Gorgonzola dolce, Valdeón, Stilton, bleu d'Auvergne, Shropshire Blue

presenting cheese

Whether served as a savory tidbit to start or finish a meal, or as the star of a casual gathering, cheese is always a versatile offering. Serve it on its own or with accompaniments—spreads, such as chutneys, jams, or tapenades; sweet elements, like honeycomb or fresh, dried, or candied fruits; or salty bites, such as olives or nuts—and a crusty baguette.

cheese plates

You can serve one carefully chosen cheese and let its extraordinary qualities shine. But, in general, an assortment of three cheeses offers variety without overwhelming guests. When making your selections, diversity can be created in different ways: cheese age or type (one bloomy rind, one semifirm, one blue); milk type (one cow's milk, one goat's milk, one sheep's milk); country of origin (one French, one Spanish, one English); or even locale (three from California). Ultimately, you'll want a range of flavors and textures, from creamy and buttery to crumbly and salty, and a mix of shapes and colors. Choose accompaniments to match the cheese, season, and occasion, keeping flavor and texture in mind.

serving

Arrange cheeses so that they are easy to cut, such as laying a wedge on its side. Consider making the first cut yourself, as a guide, slicing so that each piece will have a bit of rind. This helps avoid an empty chunk of rind at the end of serving. Always let cheese come to room temperature before eating it. This may take up to a couple of hours.

equipment

A large platter, marble slab, or wooden board can accommodate three or four cheeses. Allow ample room for easy cutting. For a more formal presentation, you can pass individual cheese boards among guests. Give each cheese its own knife, so flavors don't mingle. Rounded knives are best for spreading luscious, creamy cheeses, and sharp knives are ideal for cutting hard aged cheeses. A cheese knife with tines is perfect for transferring slices to plates.

purchasing and storing

Cheeses are best freshly cut, so avoid prewrapped pieces when possible. Storing cheese is always a balancing act: cheese must "breathe" or release moisture, but it also needs to stay moist and not dry out. Whenever possible, buy cheeses on the day of serving and keep the wedges at cool room temperature on a board or under a glass dome. When refrigerating, plastic wrap is the common, though imperfect, solution. The cheese won't breathe, but it also won't dry out. Use waxed paper for wrapping fresh and soft-ripened cheeses, which need to breathe the most in order to ripen properly.

wine and cheese pairing

When done well, a wine and cheese pairing delights the palate. Try experimenting with different combinations to discover what flavor matches appeal to you. There are no hard-set rules, only helpful guidelines and considerations that can assist you in your choice.

characteristics

Just as cheeses have very different personalities, from texture to aroma to color to flavor, so do wines. Here are the key qualities to keep in mind when pairing them.

flavor Cheese and wine flavors can match or, more often, they can pleasantly oppose and counterbalance. A citrusy Sauvignon Blanc can echo the tartness of a fresh chèvre beautifully, but a sweet dessert wine can complement a salty blue cheese as well. The flavors to look for when choosing a wine to pair with cheese are acidity or tartness (which comes from the grapes); bitterness (from the grape skins and wooden barrels used for aging); sweetness (from the residual sugar that remains after fermentation); and spiciness (the peppery flavor that some wines, such as Syrah, may display).

texture Consider whether a cheese is smooth, creamy, crumbly, firm, or hard and dry before you begin pairing. This will lead you to consider compatible qualities in your wine choice: think crisp, dry, buttery, velvety, or full-bodied.

age Match light with light, and strong with strong. In general, this means that younger, lighter wines will work best with younger, milder cheeses, while long-aged cheeses need well-aged wines.

white wines Because of their high acidity levels, white wines are a natural match for most cheeses. A wine with a buttery texture makes for pleasing cheese pairings, but almost any style of white, from crisp and dry to fruity and sweet, will find a mate. Heavily oaked Chardonnays are the exception, as they often have a bitter flavor that does not pair well with food.

red wines The right red wine is delicious when paired with the right cheese, but this tends to be a somewhat tricky matching process—and always open to personal tastes. Avoid tannic reds, which may end up tasting bitter or almost metallic when matched with cheese. Light, fruity reds are the easiest to pair. That said, a full Cabernet or even a lush ruby port can be terrific with an aged blue.

sparkling wines A simple reason explains why sparkling wines work marvelously with cheese: where cheese coats the mouth, the bright bubbles in the wine cleanse the palate, refreshing it after each bite. A creamy cheese, such as a triple-cream Brie, is an especially nice match, but salty and blue cheeses also do well with bubbles.

classic matches that work

In the best cheese and wine pairings, each enhances and balances or brings out the best flavors of the other, either by contrasting with or echoing each other. Some pairings work so well together that they have become classics, and help illustrate the interplay of wine and cheese.

chèvre and Sancerre These two specialties of the Loire Valley of central France are made for each other. The tangy, acidic flavors of fresh goat cheese can make many white wines taste bland. Crisp, lively Sauvignon Blanc (the varietal used in Sancerre) can match the cheese's acidity with its own, and its herbaceous or "grassy" quality highlights the earthiness of the cheese.

double or triple creams and Champagne Extremely rich cheeses like Brillat-Savarin coat the mouth. The bubbles and subtle fruit of a sparkling wine refresh the palate by cutting through the creaminess, yet emphasizing its luxurious texture.

CHEESE TYPES		WINE MATCHES
fresh or less-aged cheeses	young Asiago, *crescenza*, young Mahón, Humboldt Fog, feta, young *pecorino toscano*	**light, fruity, high-acid white wines** Sauvignon Blanc/Sancerre, Pinot Grigio, dry Riesling, Grüner Veltliner, Chenin Blanc/Vouvray, Albariño; dry rosés
more-aged firm cheeses	Cheshire, aged Asiago, Cantal, Cheddar, Mahón, Manchego, *pecorino toscano*	**full-bodied red wines** Cabernet Sauvignon/ Bordeaux, Merlot, Chianti, Barbaresco, Barbera, Barolo, Rhône, Languedoc, Ribera del Duero, Rioja, Sangiovese, Syrah/Shiraz, Zinfandel
	Cheddar	**port** vintage, tawny
hard well-aged cheeses	Parmigiano-Reggiano	**sparkling wines** Champagne, prosecco, *cava*
	Parmigiano-Reggiano, dry Jack, Mahón, aged Manchego	**dry sherries** *fino*, Manzanilla
aged cheeses with nutty or sweet flavors	Gruyère, Comté, raclette, Gouda, Emmentaler	**rich, lush, fragrant white wines** Chardonnay/white Burgundy, Gewürztraminer, Grüner Veltliner, late-harvest Riesling, Viognier, Chenin Blanc/Vouvray
	Gruyère, Comté, raclette, Gouda, tomme de Savoie	**light- to medium-bodied red wines** Beaujolais, Dolcetto d'Alba, Grenache, Nero d'Avola, Pinot Noir/red Burgundy
	Gruyère, Comté, Gorgonzola *naturale*, Stilton, Valdeón	**dessert wines with nutty and caramel flavor** Madeira, *vin santo*, off-dry sherries (amontillado and oloroso)
bloomy-rind cheeses	Brie, Camembert	**sparkling wines** Champagne, prosecco, *cava* **light- to medium-bodied red wines** Beaujolais, dolcetto d'Alba, Grenache, Nero d'Avola, Pinot Noir/red Burgundy

Parmigiano-Reggiano and Sangiovese

Here again, bringing together a cheese and wine from the same area can enhance the match. Hard aged cheeses with a little bite tend to pair well with red wines, and two red wines made in the same region as premier Parmigiano-Reggiano cheese are Chianti and Brunello, both from the Sangiovese grape. These rich, medium- to full-bodied wines tame the sharpness of the cheese, and the pleasantly salty cheese brings out the ripe fruit notes in the wine.

Stilton and port This famous and sublime pairing was originally brought together by the vagaries of English maritime history. English Stilton—a creamy blue with distinctive salty, nutty, meaty, and smoky flavors—meets its match in vintage port, originating in Portugal, with its equally luscious mouthfeel; sweet, ripe flavors; and full, high-octane body. The sweetness of the wine counteracts the saltiness of the cheese, and the pairing makes each bite or sip more entrancing.

CHEESE TYPES		WINE MATCHES
double- and triple-cream cheeses	Brillat-Savarin	**rich, lush, fragrant white wines** Chardonnay/white Burgundy, Gewürztraminer, Grüner Veltliner, late-harvest Riesling, Viognier, Chenin Blanc/Vouvray
washed-rind cheeses	Morbier	**sparkling wines** Champagne, prosecco, *cava*
	Morbier, Époisses de Bourgogne, Fontina, Muenster, Pont-l'Évêque, Taleggio	**rich, lush, fragrant white wines** Chardonnay/white Burgundy, Gewürztraminer, Grüner Veltliner, late-harvest Riesling, Viognier, Chenin Blanc/Vouvray
	Fontina, Pont-l'Évêque, Taleggio	**light- to medium-bodied red wines** Beaujolais, Dolcetto d'Alba, Grenache, Nero d'Avola, Pinot Noir/Burgundy
	Taleggio	**full-bodied red wines** Cabernet Sauvignon/Bordeaux, Merlot, Chianti, Barbaresco, Barbera, Barolo, Rhône, Languedoc, Ribera del Duero, Rioja, Sangiovese, Syrah/Shiraz, Zinfandel
blue cheeses	bleu d'Auvergne, Cashel blue, Fourme d'Ambert, Roquefort	**dessert wines** Sauternes, late-harvest Sauvignon Blanc
mild to medium-intensity blue cheeses	Cashel blue, Fourme d'Ambert, Gorgonzola *dolce*	**sparkling wines** Champagne, prosecco, *cava*
buttery blue cheeses	Stilton, Cashel blue	**off-dry sherries** amontadillo, oloroso
powerful blue cheeses	Gorgonzola *naturale*, Stilton, Valdeón	**dessert wines** Madeira, *vin santo,* off-dry sherries (amontillado and oloroso), vintage or tawny port, Sauternes

beer and cheese pairing

Although many among the food-world elite insist that wine and cheese are the ideal partners, some contend that beer and cheese are the true soul mates. In earlier times, beer and cheese were commonly made by the same person, or at least in the same setting: on the farm. Today, cheeses made in areas with celebrated breweries are classically paired with beer.

characteristics

Wine and cheese combinations are often outstanding, of course, but they can also be disappointing or worse. That's because the best marriages typically rely on contrasting flavors, which can be difficult to match successfully. Pairing beer and cheese is usually much easier, because their flavors tend to complement each other. This is particularly true of malty beers, such as ale, porter, and stout, which include many of the same nutty caramel flavors found in aged cheeses. And the highly flavored washed-rind cheeses, which are especially challenging to pair with wine without overpowering the wine, meet their match with beer, often one made in the same area.

malty with nutty Mellow, malty beers tend to be predominantly sweet, pairing best with nutty or caramel-toned cheeses. Try a malty amber or brown ale with a Gruyère, Gouda, or Asiago.

light with light Dry, delicate lagers, particularly pilsners, call for younger, milder cheeses. But do not assume that the inverse is always true. Pairing an intense beer with an intense cheese may end in an unpleasant clash of the Titans.

bitter with sharp Particularly hoppy, bitter beers call for sharp, biting cheeses. Pair a single or double IPA with an aged Cheddar or Cheshire. The strong hops and high alcohol content of the pale ale make a great match for a tart cheese.

carbonation One of the main reasons that beer and cheese pair well is the carbonation. All beers are carbonated, which means they work as palate cleansers, not unlike Champagne or other sparkling wines. After enjoying a mouth-coating bite of cheese, a sip of beer refreshes you for the next morsel. This is particularly true for creamier cheeses and fizzier varieties of beer: try a luscious soft goat cheese with a bright, light-bodied hefeweizen.

other beer flavors Porters and stouts offer bold flavor, featuring cocoa or espresso tones. These brews work well with many soft-ripened and pungent washed-rind cheeses. Even feisty blue cheeses, which defy many attempted wine pairings, can find a good partner here: the right dark beer makes a felicitous match with a Stilton.

the cheese
course

Whether at my home in Winters or at my
farmhouse in Provence, a cheese course is a part
of my daily meal, preceding it in California and
following it in France. Sometimes it's as simple as a wedge
of pungent blue drizzled with honey, or a round of creamy
chèvre served with local walnuts and apricots. When my
French son-in-law is at the table, I like to spoil him with
a selection of cheeses paired with accompaniments,
like warm dates, berry compote, or citrusy olives.

spring cheese plates

In spring, cheeses are particularly mild, thanks to the animals' diet of tender greens. Assemble a trio of cheeses made from different milks, or showcase two soft, creamy cheeses alongside cherries to celebrate the season. A dry Bandol-style rosé will complement either plate.

apricots, almonds, and a trio of cheeses

6–8 oz (185–250 g) fresh goat's milk cheese

6–8 oz (185–250 g) sheep's milk cheese such as *pecorino pepato*

6–8 oz (185–250 g) semifirm cow's milk cheese such as tomme de Savoie

2 apricots or peaches, thinly sliced

½ cup (3 oz/90 g) almonds

About 2 hours before serving, remove the cheeses from the refrigerator, unwrap them, and allow them to come to room temperature.

When ready to serve, arrange the cheeses, apricot slices, and almonds on a cutting board, marble slab, or platter. Include a spreader for the soft cheese and a paring knife for each of the other cheeses. Serve with baguette rounds, thin slices of dark bread, or crackers, if desired.

cherries with triple-cream cheeses

2 triple-cream cheeses, 6–8 oz (185–250 g) *each*, such as La Tur or Mt Tam

6–8 oz (185–250 g) soft-ripened cow's milk cheese such as Brie

½ lb (8 oz/250 g) cherries

About 2 hours before serving, remove the cheeses from the refrigerator, unwrap them, and allow them to come to room temperature.

When ready to serve, arrange the cheeses and cherries on a cutting board, marble slab, or platter. Include a paring knife or soft-cheese knife for each cheese. Serve with baguette rounds, thin slices of dark bread, or crackers, if desired.

summer cheese plates

A selection of flavorful cheeses, a big green salad, and a crisp white wine make a light and easy summer meal. I like to pair an aromatic cheese, like an Alsatian Muenster, with a nuttier hard type. For a Provençal touch, drizzle goat cheese with a fruity olive oil and top with fresh herbs.

seasonal fruit and flavorful cheeses

6–8 oz (185–250 g) hard sheep's milk cheese such as pecorino

6–8 oz (185–250 g) washed-rind cheese such as Muenster or Taleggio

3–4 oz (90–125 g) fresh goat's milk cheese

3–4 oz (90–125 g) blue cheese such as Cabrales

2 peaches, apples, or apricots, thinly sliced

½ cup (2 oz/60 g) walnuts or Marcona almonds

Extra-virgin olive oil and fresh rosemary sprigs

About 2 hours before serving, remove the cheeses from the refrigerator, unwrap them, and allow them to come to room temperature.

When ready to serve, arrange the cheeses, fruit, and nuts on a cutting board, marble slab, or platter. Place the goat cheese in a small dish, drizzle with the olive oil, and top with the rosemary. Include a spreader for the soft cheese, paring knives for the washed-rind and blue, and a sharp paring knife or cheese plane for the hard cheese. Serve with baguette rounds, thin slices of dark bread, or crackers, if desired.

nectarines, honey, pistachios, and fresh cheeses

6–8 oz (185–250 g) fresh goat's milk cheese

6–8 oz (185–250 g) fresh mozzarella cheese

6–8 oz (185–250 g) soft cow's milk cheese such as Banon

2 nectarines, thinly sliced

½ cup (2 oz/60 g) pistachios

Honey

About 2 hours before serving, remove the cheeses from the refrigerator, unwrap them, and allow them to come to room temperature.

When ready to serve, arrange the cheeses, nectarine slices, and pistachios on a cutting board, marble slab, or platter. Place the honey in a small dish. Include a spreader or paring knife for each soft cheese. Serve with baguette rounds, thin slices of dark bread, or crackers, if desired.

the cheese course   29

fall and winter cheese plates

SERVES 4–6

During the cooler months, I like to serve richer, more aged cheeses. Seasonal fruits like figs, pomegranates, grapes, pears, and persimmons add a bright and flavorful juiciness to any cheese plate. Pour a Rhône, Rioja, Chianti, or other medium-bodied red wine for either plate.

pomegranates, figs, pecans, and aged cheeses

6–8 oz (185–250 g) aged goat's milk cheese such as Garrotxa

6–8 oz (185–250 g) washed-rind cow's milk cheese such as Red Hawk or Saint-Nectaire

6–8 oz (185–250 g) triple-cream cheese such as La Tur or Brillat-Savarin

1 pomegranate, pulled apart into pieces

4 fresh figs

½ cup (2 oz/60 g) pecans or hazelnuts, toasted

About 2 hours before serving, remove the cheeses from the refrigerator, unwrap them, and allow them to come to room temperature.

When ready to serve, arrange the cheeses, pomegranate, figs, and pecans on a cutting board, marble slab, or platter. Include a spreader for each soft cheese and a sharp paring knife or cheese plane for the hard cheese. Serve with baguette rounds, thin slices of dark bread, or crackers, if desired.

persimmons, dates, and soft cheeses

2 soft cheeses, 6–8 oz (185–250 g) *each*, such as Camembert, chèvre, or Monte Enebro

6–8 oz (185–250 g) triple-cream cheese such as La Tur or Explorateur

2 persimmons, very thinly sliced

½ cup (3 oz/90 g) dates

½ cup (2½ oz/75 g) cashews

About 2 hours before serving, remove the cheeses from the refrigerator, unwrap them, and allow them to come to room temperature.

When ready to serve, arrange the cheeses, persimmon slices, dates, and cashews on a cutting board, marble slab, or platter. Include a paring knife or soft-cheese knife for each cheese. Serve with baguette rounds, thin slices of dark bread, or crackers, if desired.

beer-friendly cheese plates

Pairing beer and cheese can yield a sharp and tangy marriage. A pungent, washed-rind cow's milk cheese such as Fontina, aged Gouda, or Appenzeller, is a terrific choice, as are mild blues and any style of Cheddar. Nuts, pickles, and dried fruit enhance the hops in beer.

stilton, walnuts, and dried fruits

6–8 oz (185–250 g) aged Gouda such as Saenkanter or UnieKaas

6–8 oz (185–250 g) aged goat's milk cheese such as Crottin de Chavignol

6–8 oz (185–250 g) mild blue-veined cheese such as Stilton

1 cup (6 oz/185 g) dates

Dried fruits such as persimmons, apricots, and pears

½ cup (2 oz/60 g) walnuts

About 2 hours before serving, remove the cheeses from the refrigerator, unwrap them, and allow them to come to room temperature.

When ready to serve, arrange the cheeses, dates, dried fruit, and nuts on a cutting board, marble slab, or platter. Include paring knives for the blue and the crottin and a sharp paring knife or cheese plane for the Gouda. Serve with baguette rounds, thin slices of dark bread, or crackers, if desired.

farmstead cheddar, pears, and chutney

6–8 oz (185–250 g) farmstead Cheddar cheese

6–8 oz (185–250 g) hard cow's milk cheese such as Mimolette or dry Jack

6–8 oz (185–250 g) hard sheep's milk cheese such as *pecorino sardo*

2 pears, thinly sliced

¼ cup (2½ oz/75 g) apricot chutney

About 2 hours before serving, remove the cheeses from the refrigerator, unwrap them, and allow them to come to room temperature.

When ready to serve, arrange the cheeses, pears, and chutney on a cutting board, marble slab, or platter. Include a paring knife or cheese plane for the cheeses. Serve with baguette rounds, thin slices of dark bread, or crackers, if desired.

cranberry-pear chutney

MAKES 3 CUPS
(30 oz/940 g)

Fruit chutney flavored with aromatic spices pairs well with almost any type of cheese, young or aged. Both cow's milk and aged sheep's milk cheeses are good choices, but this tangy chutney is also superb served slathered atop fresh ricotta or soft goat cheese.

1 cup (6 oz/185 g) minced white onion

1 cup (8 fl oz/250 ml) apple cider

¾ cup (6 fl oz/180 ml) fresh orange juice

2 Tbsp cider vinegar

4 juniper berries

1 Tbsp coarsely grated lemon zest

1 Tbsp coarsely grated orange zest

1 cinnamon stick, 1½ inches (4 cm) long

6 whole cloves

1¼ cups (9 oz/280 g) firmly packed light brown sugar

1 bag (12 oz/375 g) fresh cranberries (about 3 cups)

2 Bosc or other firm but ripe pears, peeled, halved, cored, and cut into 1-inch (2.5-cm) cubes

In a nonreactive saucepan, combine the onion, apple cider, orange juice, cider vinegar, juniper berries, lemon zest, orange zest, cinnamon stick, and cloves. Bring to a boil over medium-high heat, reduce the heat to medium, and cook, uncovered, stirring occasionally, until reduced to 1½ cups (12 fl oz/375 ml), 10–15 minutes.

Stir in the brown sugar until it dissolves, about 2 minutes. Add the cranberries and pears and return to a boil. Reduce the heat to low and simmer, uncovered, stirring occasionally, until the flavors have blended, 20–30 minutes. The fruit will be quite soft.

Pour the chutney into a jar or bowl and stir with a fork, crushing some, but not all, of the fruit. Let cool completely before serving. The chutney can be tightly covered and refrigerated for up to 1 week. Bring to room temperature before serving.

serve with cheese
Parmigiano-Reggiano, aged pecorino, Taleggio, soft goat cheese, or Camembert

serve with wine
A medium-bodied red such as Barbera or Côtes du Rhône

warm marinated olives

MAKES 1½ CUPS
(7 oz / 220 g)

A homemade marinade personalizes cured olives, heightening their appeal. Serve as is, or warm them to release a bouquet of heady aromas. For cheese pairings, look to the Mediterranean: sheep's and cow's milk cheeses from Spain, France, and Greece partner perfectly with olives.

1 cup (5 oz/155 g) assorted olives such as Picholine, Niçoise, and Kalamata

½ cup (4 fl oz/125 ml) extra-virgin olive oil

½ tsp fennel seeds, coarsely crushed

1 orange peel strip, about 2 inches (5 cm) long

1 Tbsp fresh lemon juice

Rinse the olives well and pat thoroughly dry. In a frying pan over medium heat, warm the olive oil. When the oil is hot, stir in the olives, fennel seeds, and orange peel and heat until the olives are hot throughout, about 2 minutes. Remove from the heat, transfer to a bowl, and let cool completely.

Add the lemon juice to the olives and toss well. Cover and let stand at room temperature for at least 8 hours or up to 24 hours, stirring occasionally to redistribute the seasoning. (At this point, the olives can be refrigerated for up to 2 weeks before serving.)

To serve, preheat the oven to 350°F (180°C). Put the olives and their marinade in a baking dish and bake until they are warm throughout, about 10 minutes. Using a slotted spoon, lift the olives out of the marinade and transfer to a serving dish. Serve warm, with a bowl alongside for pits.

serve with cheese
Manchego, Cantal, Istara, or feta

serve with wine
A crisp white such as Albariño or smooth red such as Malbec

artichoke hearts
with citrus zest

MAKES 2 CUPS
(10 oz / 315 g)

Since I'm blessed with a dozen artichoke plants in my garden, I prefer to use fresh artichoke hearts when possible. This little antipasto is an exception, however. It tastes fantastic and is very easy to make on short notice. For the marinade, use fresh citrus and a good, fruity olive oil.

1 jar (12 oz/375 g)
water-packed
artichoke hearts

3 Tbsp extra-virgin olive oil

Grated zest of 1 lemon

2 tsp fresh lemon juice

1 tsp minced fresh
flat-leaf parsley

½ tsp sea salt

1–1½ tsp mixed red
and black peppercorns

2 Tbsp capers or small
caper berries, rinsed

Drain and rinse the artichoke hearts, then pat dry. If the hearts are whole, cut into quarters lengthwise. Set aside.

In a large bowl, stir together the olive oil, lemon zest, lemon juice, parsley, salt, peppercorns, and capers with a fork. Add the artichoke hearts and turn gently to coat. Cover and let stand at room temperature for 1 hour, then cover and refrigerate for at least 24 hours or up to 3 days to allow the flavors to blend. Bring to room temperature before serving.

serve with cheese
Boucheron, Banon, or feta

serve with wine
A light white such as Sauvignon Blanc, Vermentino, or Sancerre

toasted nuts

Toasting brings out the flavor of nuts, gilding their color and adding crunch. Cheeses with a nutty flavor, like Beaufort, pair well with both almonds and walnuts, while Stilton is a classic with walnuts. Serve with a cluster of grapes or slices of pear or apple.

1 lb (500 g)
walnuts or almonds

1 Tbsp sea salt

2 Tbsp minced fresh
rosemary (optional)

Preheat the oven to 350°F (180°C). In a bowl, mix together the nuts, salt, and rosemary, if using.

Spread the nuts in a single layer on a rimmed baking sheet. Place in the oven and toast, stirring several times, until fragrant and starting to turn golden, about 10 minutes. Pour onto paper towels and let cool to room temperature.

Transfer to a bowl to serve. The nuts will keep, stored in an airtight container at room temperature, for up to 1 week.

serve with cheese
Brie, Camembert, Beaufort, Cantal, Emmentaler, Cheddar, or Stilton

serve with wine or beer
A light-bodied red or white or a light beer

glazed cipolline

MAKES 1½ CUPS
(10 oz / 315 g)

If you like the taste of smoky chipotle chiles, you'll love these bite-sized citrus-and-chile-scented onions. I use them as often as I use my homemade pickles (page 44), as an accompaniment to cheese plates, tucked into sandwiches, or as part of a mixed antipasto.

30 cipolline onions, about 1–1½ inches (2.5–4 cm) in diameter, or pearl onions

3 lbsp unsalted butter

¼ cup (2 fl oz/60 ml) fresh orange juice

½ canned chipotle chile in adobo sauce, seeded and minced

Bring a saucepan three-fourths full of water to a boil over high heat. Add the onions and blanch for 2 minutes to loosen the papery skins. Drain and rinse under running cold water. Slip off the skins, then trim only the tip of each root, leaving the base intact. This helps the onions hold their shape during cooking.

In a sauté pan just large enough to hold the onions in a single layer, melt the butter over medium-high heat. When it foams, add the onions and cook, stirring often, until lightly golden, about 12 minutes. Add ¼ cup (2 fl oz/60 ml) water, the orange juice, and the chile and stir well. Bring to a boil, reduce the heat to low, cover, and simmer until the onions are tender and glazed and most of the liquid has been absorbed, 10–15 minutes longer.

Transfer the onions to a bowl and let cool. Cover and refrigerate for up to 1 week before using. Bring to room temperature before serving.

serve with cheese
A firm, salty cheese such as feta, dry Jack, or sharp Cheddar, or a semifirm Monterey Jack

serve with wine or beer
Cabernet Sauvignon, Syrah, or Zinfandel for red, Pinot Grigio for white, or brown ale

oven-roasted tomatoes

Prepare these succulent plum tomatoes year-round to capture a hit of fresh tomato flavor. (In summer, when tomatoes are at their peak, substitute heirloom or toy box varieties.) Serve them alongside mozzarella, ricotta, or other soft, mild cheeses, or as a crostini topping.

¼ cup (2 fl oz/60 ml)
extra-virgin olive oil,
plus more for greasing

4–5 lb (2–2.5 kg) plum
tomatoes, halved lengthwise

Sea salt

Preheat the oven to 400°F (200°C). Oil 2 rimmed baking sheets.

Lay the tomatoes, cut side up, in a single layer on the prepared baking sheet. Brush with the ¼ cup olive oil and sprinkle with ½ teaspoon salt. Roast until the tomatoes are slightly shrunken, about 20 minutes. Reduce the heat to 225°F (110°C) and continue to roast until the tomatoes have softened, collapsed onto themselves, and are slightly caramelized, about 2 hours longer.

Remove from the oven and let cool to room temperature. Season to taste with salt, then serve.

serve with cheese
Soft, mild cheeses enhance the tomato flavor; try *burrata*, mozzarella, Teleme, or goat cheese

serve with wine
Think Italian: Pinot Grigio, Vernaccia, or Vermentino for white; Sangiovese, Barbera, or Chianti for red

quick pickles

The ploughman's lunch—aged cheese, pickles, and country bread—is a staple of British public-house menus. Here, spring vegetables are soaked in a simple brine to yield crunchy pub-worthy pickles that pair perfectly with a crumbly Cheddar and a pint of beer.

1 lb (500 g) mixed vegetables, such as okra, carrots, green beans, red onions, beets, asparagus, and/or radishes

1 cup (8 fl oz/250 ml) white wine vinegar

1 Tbsp kosher salt

2 bay leaves

2 cloves garlic

2 tsp mustard seeds

2 tsp peppercorns

Have ready two 1-pint (16–fl oz/500-ml) jars. Trim the vegetables, making sure the okra, carrots, and green beans are ½ inch (12 mm) shorter than the height of the jars, and slicing or quartering the onions, beets, and radishes to easily fit.

In a small saucepan, combine 1 cup (8 fl oz/250 ml) water, the vinegar, and the salt. Bring to a boil over medium-high heat, stirring occasionally to dissolve the salt.

Place 1 bay leaf, 1 garlic clove, and 1 teaspoon *each* mustard seeds and peppercorns in each jar. Divide the vegetables in half and pack half into each jar, making sure they reach no higher than within ½ inch (12 mm) of the rim. Ladle the hot brine over the vegetables, leaving ½ inch (12 mm) headspace. Let cool completely, then cover tightly and refrigerate for at least 24 hours before serving to allow the flavors to blend. The pickles will keep for up to 1 week.

serve with cheese
A sharp, aged farmhouse Cheddar, Cheshire, or Stilton

serve with wine or beer
A medium-bodied Cabernet Sauvignon, crisp Sauvignon Blanc, or hoppy, dry IPA

meyer lemon and green olive relish

MAKES 1 CUP
(8 oz / 250 g)

This tangy relish reminds me of a lemony tapenade. I like to serve a dollop of it on top of crackers with thin slices of soft goat cheese, either as an appetizer or as part of a cheese plate. For a hearty bite that emphasizes the buttery flesh of the olives, spoon it on top of Cheddar.

2 Meyer lemons, quartered lengthwise and seeded

1 shallot, coarsely chopped

2 Tbsp finely chopped fresh flat-leaf parsley

½ cup (3 oz/90 g) pitted green olives

1 tsp coriander seeds

1 tsp white balsamic vinegar

¼ tsp sea salt

¼ tsp freshly ground white pepper

Scoop out about half of the pulp from each lemon quarter and discard. Coarsely chop the lemon quarters, then put them in a food processor or blender. Add the shallot, parsley, and olives and pulse several times until minced but not puréed. Transfer to a bowl and stir in the coriander seeds and vinegar. Season with the salt and pepper. For a chunkier relish, chop the olives coarsely by hand and stir them into the minced lemon mixture with the coriander and vinegar.

Serve at once, or cover and refrigerate for up to 3 days. Bring to room temperature before serving.

serve with cheese
Pecorino or other semifirm sheep's milk cheese, aged Asiago, farmstead Cheddar, or goat cheese

serve with wine
Viognier or Grüner Veltliner for white, or Zinfandel or Syrah for red

cherry compote

MAKES 1 CUP
(8 oz/250 g)

Quick and easy to make, this vibrant compote goes well with a wide range of cheeses. I like it with mild, soft cheeses, such as ricotta, and with sharp Cheddars. It's also excellent with Humboldt Fog, a goat cheese with a layer of ash that's made not far from my California home.

½ cup (4 oz/125 g) sugar

1 cup (6 oz/185 g) pitted and stemmed sweet cherries

2 tsp fresh lemon juice

¼ tsp almond extract

In a small saucepan, combine the sugar and ½ cup (4 fl oz/125 ml) water. Place over low heat and bring to a simmer, stirring, until the sugar dissolves. Add the cherries and cook just until they are warmed through, about 5 minutes. Transfer to a bowl and stir in the lemon juice and almond extract. Let cool to room temperature.

Serve at once, or cover and refrigerate for up to 3 days. Bring to room temperature before serving.

serve with cheese
Parmigiano-Reggiano, aged pecorino, sharp Cheddar, or crottin

serve with wine
Pinot Noir, Cabernet Franc, or dolcetto

sherried figs

Figs, both fresh and dried, are classic accompaniments to cheese. Sherry and sugar enhance the natural sweetness of dried figs and make them an outstanding match for blue cheeses and aged cheeses. I serve these figs as a starter, part of a cheese plate, or even a light dessert.

1 cup (8 fl oz/250 ml) dry sherry

2 Tbsp sugar

12 dried figs such as Calimyrna or Smyrna

In a saucepan, combine the sherry, sugar, and 1 cup (8 fl oz/250 ml) water. Place over medium heat, bring to a boil, reduce the heat to low, and add the figs. Simmer, uncovered, until the figs are plump and soft, about 10 minutes.

Remove from the heat. Using a slotted spoon, transfer the figs to a plate. Trim off the hard tip of each stem, then cut in half or leave whole. Serve warm or at room temperature. Or, transfer the figs and their cooking syrup to a covered container and refrigerate for up to 5 days. Trim as directed and then bring to room temperature before serving.

serve with cheese
Blues such as Cabrales or Danish, or hard aged cheeses such as Jack or Parmigiano-Reggiano

serve with wine
A medium-bodied red, *vin santo,* or sherry

grape focaccia

The surprising addition of fresh grapes to classic focaccia adds color, flavor, and juiciness. The slightly sweet taste of the grapes makes the bread especially good to serve with medium to sharp cheeses, where the sweetness provides a counterpoint to the character of the cheese.

1 package (2½ tsp) active dry yeast

2 cups (10 oz/315 g) all-purpose flour, plus more as needed

½ tsp fine sea salt

2 Tbsp extra-virgin olive oil, plus more for brushing

1 cup (6 oz/185 g) seedless green or red grapes, or a mixture, halved

Coarse sea salt for sprinkling

In a large bowl, dissolve the yeast in ¾ cup (6 fl oz/180 ml) warm water (110°F /43°C) and let stand until foamy, about 5 minutes. Using a wooden spoon, stir in the flour, fine sea salt, and 2 tablespoons olive oil to make a soft dough. Turn the dough out onto a lightly floured work surface and knead, adding more flour as needed, until soft, smooth, and slightly sticky, about 10 minutes. Form into a ball, transfer to a lightly oiled bowl, turn to coat, and cover with a damp kitchen towel or plastic wrap. Let rise in a warm, draft-free place until doubled in bulk, about 1 hour.

Lightly oil an 8-inch (20-cm) square pan or a small baking sheet. Turn the dough out onto a lightly floured work surface and knead in the grapes. Transfer the dough to the prepared pan. Using your fingers, stretch it to cover the bottom of the square pan evenly or into a roughly 10-inch (25-cm) oval on the baking sheet. Cover loosely with a kitchen towel and let rise in a warm, draft-free place until doubled, about 1 hour.

Preheat the oven to 400°F (200°C). Brush the dough with oil and sprinkle with coarse salt. Dimple the dough with your fingertips. Bake until lightly browned, 35–45 minutes. Transfer to a wire rack and let cool for 5–10 minutes. Cut into pieces and serve.

serve with cheese
Cheddar, Fontina, *grana padano*, dry Jack, or aged pecorino

serve with wine
Chianti, Sangiovese, Barbera, or Nebbiolo

starters

My daughter-in-law has been learning to
make cheese at her small homestead in Northern
California, and I am the lucky beneficiary. She brings me
samples of her Camembert and hand-pulled mozzarella,
as well as crocks of her deliciously tart and tangy lightly
peppered goat cheese. For an easy starter, I like to slather
her homemade chèvre on crostini, then add chopped
kumquats and fresh thyme, both picked in the garden
that lies just outside my kitchen door.

burrata with grilled bread and heirloom tomatoes

SERVES 4–6

Whenever I can find *burrata*—a mozzarella-type Italian cheese with a creamy center—I make these toasts. Thankfully, it's now offered by a few domestic producers and is easier to locate than it used to be. In winter, substitute oil-packed sun-dried tomatoes for the heirlooms.

¼ cup (2 fl oz/60 ml) extra-virgin olive oil, plus more as needed

1 baguette, thinly sliced on the diagonal

4 cloves garlic, halved lengthwise

About 1½ lb (750 g) heirloom tomatoes in a variety of sizes and colors

1 ball *burrata* cheese, about 10 oz (315 g)

Sea salt and freshly ground pepper

Preheat a grill to medium-high and oil the grill rack.

Brush the baguette slices on both sides with the ¼ cup olive oil. Place on the hot grill and grill the baguette slices until golden on the first side, about 3 minutes. Turn and grill on the second side until golden, 2–3 minutes longer. Transfer to a platter and rub the top side of each toast with the cut side of a garlic clove.

Depending on their size, thinly slice the tomatoes or cut into halves or narrow wedges. Arrange the *burrata*, tomatoes, and grilled bread on a serving platter, set out containers of olive oil and salt and pepper, and let guests assemble their own toasts. Alternatively, arrange the toasts on a platter, place some tomato on each toast, and sprinkle with salt and pepper. Top with some *burrata* and a drizzle of olive oil. Serve right away.

try different cheeses
Buffalo mozzarella or soft goat cheese

serve with wine
Southern Italian varietals such as Falanghina for white or Nero d'Avola for red

warm dates with parmesan and walnuts

SERVES 6–8

Winter is date season, and I look forward to the new crop each year, particularly meaty Medjools. I like to pair the dense, sweet fruit with salty Parmesan and earthy, crunchy walnuts. You can assemble this easy appetizer up to 8 hours in advance and heat just before serving.

24 large dates,
preferably Medjool

2 tsp extra-virgin olive oil
or walnut oil, plus more
for drizzling

2-oz (60-g) piece
Parmesan cheese, preferably
Parmigiano-Reggiano

24 walnut halves

Preheat the oven to 350°F (180°C).

Using a paring knife, make a small, lengthwise incision in each date and carefully remove the pit. In a bowl, gently toss the pitted dates with the 2 teaspoons olive oil. Arrange the dates, slit side up, in a single layer on a rimmed baking sheet or in a shallow baking dish. Using a vegetable peeler, cut the cheese into bite-sized shavings. Tuck a cheese shaving or two and a walnut half into each date.

Bake until warmed through, about 10 minutes. Transfer to a serving platter, drizzle with more olive oil, and serve at once.

try different cheeses
Pecorino or soft goat cheese

serve with wine
Pinot Noir or sparkling wine such as prosecco

grilled nectarines with soft cheese

SERVES 4

When nectarines are grilled, they caramelize slightly and lose a bit of their tartness. A ripe, soft cheese with a near-oozing center, such as Brie or Camembert, or a triple-cream cheese like Brillat-Savarin, makes a delicate pairing for stone fruits. This dish is one of my summertime favorites.

4 nectarines

2 Tbsp extra-virgin olive oil

6 oz (185 g) soft cheese (see note)

Preheat a grill to medium-high and oil the grill rack.

Cut each nectarine in half and remove the pit. Brush the nectarine halves with the olive oil. Place on the hot grill and grill, turning once or twice, until lightly marked and the surface of the fruit begins to caramelize, about 5 minutes. (Alternatively, preheat the oven to 450°F/230°C. Arrange the nectarine halves in a single layer in a shallow baking dish and roast, turning several times, until shiny and juicy, 5–7 minutes.)

To serve, arrange 2 grilled nectarine halves on each individual plate. Divide the cheese equally among the plates and serve at once.

serving idea
Slice small wedges of cheese and serve alongside the fruit or, if the cheese is particularly ripe, scoop spoonfuls into the cavities of the nectarine halves.

serve with wine
Rosé, Sauvignon Blanc, or sparkling wine, such as prosecco or *cava*

baked soft-ripened cheese with dried fruits

SERVES 4–6

Triple-cream cheeses like Explorateur, Délice de Saint-Cyr, or Boursault are fantastic when baked. Soaking the accompanying fruit in rum adds flavor and brings out the tanginess of the cheese. I live in an apricot-growing region, but dried peaches, pears, or nectarines would be good, too.

¼ cup (1½ oz/45 g) golden raisins

¼ cup (1½ oz/45 g) dark raisins

2–4 dried apricots, minced

½ cup (4 fl oz/125 ml) dark or light rum

1 round or wedge of soft-ripened cheese (see note), about 3 inches (7.5 cm) in diameter and 2 inches (5 cm) thick

1 baguette, sliced, for serving

In a bowl, combine the raisins and apricots with the rum, cover, and let stand for 24 hours at room temperature.

Drain, reserving the rum, now sweetened with the flavor of the fruit, for another use. Pat the fruit dry. Place the cheese in a small baking dish. Mound the plumped fruits on top of the cheese, pressing them to make sure they adhere, and around the sides. Refrigerate for 15 minutes. Preheat the oven to 425°F (220°C).

Bake until the cheese is warmed through, about 10 minutes. Serve at once, accompanied by the baguette slices.

try different cheeses
Brie, Camembert, or Brillat-Savarin

serve with wine
Chardonnay, Bordeaux, or Cabernet Sauvignon, or a dessert wine such as Sauternes or Muscat

blue cheese, fig, and walnut tartlets

Nearly any type of blue cheese can be used to make these tartlets. The trick is to add enough half-and-half or milk to make a spreadable paste that will cover the pastry smoothly. I like to use bleu d'Auvergne, which is moderately strong in flavor and blends well with the splash of dairy.

12–14 soft fresh figs

All-purpose flour for dusting

1 sheet frozen puff pastry, about ½ lb (250 g), thawed according to package instructions

6 oz (185 g) blue cheese, at room temperature

2 Tbsp half-and-half or whole milk, or as needed to create a spreadable paste

¼ cup (1 oz/30 g) finely chopped walnuts

½ tsp freshly ground pepper

½ tsp minced fresh thyme

1 tsp extra-virgin olive oil

Preheat the oven to 375°F (190°C). Trim off the hard tip from each fig stem. Cut the figs lengthwise into slices ¼ inch (6 mm) thick.

On a lightly floured work surface, roll out the puff pastry into a rectangle about 10 by 12 inches (25 by 30 cm) and about ¼ inch (6 mm) thick. Using a pastry cutter about 5 inches (13 cm) in diameter, cut out 4 rounds. Line a rimmed baking sheet with parchment paper. Transfer each pastry round to the prepared pan and, using your thumb and forefinger, lightly crimp the pastry edges to form a rim.

In a small bowl, using a fork, mash together the cheese and half-and-half, and then mix in the walnuts. Spread one-fourth of the cheese mixture over the bottom of each tartlet shell. Arrange the fig slices on top in a single layer, overlapping them slightly. Sprinkle with the pepper and thyme, and drizzle with the olive oil. Place the tartlets in the freezer for 10 minutes to help the pastry puff nicely when it bakes.

Bake the tartlets until the crust is lightly golden and the figs are soft, 15–20 minutes. Transfer to a rack to cool for about 15 minutes. Remove the tartlets from the pan and serve warm or at room temperature.

serve with wine
A sweet dessert wine such as Sauternes or full-bodied red like Zinfandel, Syrah, or Sangiovese

gorgonzola dip with crudités

Many kinds of Gorgonzola cheese are available, some creamier than others. I use Gorgonzola *dolce*, the creamiest variety, to make this flavorful dip. Serve with a selection of colorful seasonal vegetables, such as radishes and asparagus in spring or zucchini and sugar snap peas in summer.

16 thin asparagus spears, tough ends removed

8 medium or 12 baby radishes with some green leaves attached

8 medium or 4 small carrots

1 cup (3 oz/90 g) cauliflower florets

12 green onions (optional)

5 oz (155 g) soft, creamy Gorgonzola cheese (see note)

¼ cup (2 fl oz/60 ml) heavy cream, or as needed

¼ tsp freshly ground pepper

Bring water to a boil in a steamer pan. Arrange the asparagus on the steamer rack, place over the boiling water, cover, and steam until tender-crisp, about 4 minutes. Remove the asparagus from the steamer and let cool completely. Cut the spears in half on the diagonal.

Slice the radishes thinly crosswise, cut lengthwise into quarters, or leave whole, depending on their size. Peel the carrots. Halve small carrots lengthwise; halve larger carrots crosswise and then in half again lengthwise. Break or cut the cauliflower florets into small pieces. Trim the root ends and tough green tops off the green onions, if using.

In a small bowl, using a fork, mash together the cheese and cream, adding more cream if needed to make a good dipping consistency. Stir in the pepper and transfer to a small serving bowl.

Arrange the vegetables on a platter and serve the dip alongside.

serving idea
Use as a sandwich spread, paired with roast beef, prosciutto, or serrano ham.

serve with wine
Champagne, prosecco, or *cava*

cheesy artichoke dip

SERVES 6–8

Parmesan is versatile, and I always keep a big hunk of it on hand in my refrigerator. Here, the cheese adds a nutty flavor and helps to bind the artichoke hearts with the other ingredients. The result is a light and tangy dip that's quick and easy to prepare. Serve it with crostini or crackers.

1 jar (12 oz/375 g) water-packed artichoke hearts

1½ Tbsp unsalted butter, at room temperature

¾ cup (3 oz/90 g) freshly grated Parmesan cheese, preferably Parmigiano-Reggiano

¼ tsp freshly ground pepper, plus more to taste

1 Tbsp finely grated lemon zest

2 tsp fresh lemon juice

Sea salt

2 Tbsp small capers, rinsed

Drain and rinse the artichoke hearts, then pat dry and coarsely chop. In a food processor, combine the artichoke hearts, butter, Parmesan, ¼ teaspoon pepper, and lemon zest and juice. Process to a paste.

Transfer the mixture to a bowl and season with salt and more pepper, if needed. Garnish with the capers and serve at once, or cover and refrigerate for up to 1 week.

try different cheeses
Aged pecorino or *grana padano*

serve with wine
Sauvignon Blanc or sparkling wine such as *cava*

cheese and chile dip

SERVES 4–6

My family loves this simple dip, which is both creamy and spicy.
We serve it with crackers and tortilla chips, as well as celery, jicama,
and carrot sticks. My local Latin market carries the dry, piquant Cotija,
a cow's milk cheese from Michoacán, Mexico.

2 red bell peppers

1 Anaheim chile

½ cup (4 oz/125 g)
crème fraîche

½ cup (4 oz/125 g)
sour cream

½ cup (2½ oz/75 g)
crumbled Cotija cheese

1 jalapeño chile
or 2 serrano chiles,
including seeds, stemmed
and minced

¼ white onion,
minced (about 3 Tbsp)

¼ tsp cayenne pepper

¼ tsp ground cumin

Sea salt

Preheat the broiler.

Arrange the bell peppers and Anaheim chile on a small rimmed baking
sheet, slide under the broiler, and broil, turning as needed, until blistered
and charred on all sides. Transfer the peppers and chile to a resealable
plastic bag, seal closed, and let cool. When cool enough to handle,
remove the peppers and chile from the bag and peel away the charred
skin with your fingertips. Slit the pepper and chile lengthwise, discard the
seeds and ribs, and chop the flesh finely.

In a bowl, combine the crème fraîche, sour cream, cheese, jalapeño chile,
and roasted peppers and Anaheim chile and mix well. Stir in the onion,
cayenne, and cumin. Season with salt.

Serve at once, or cover and refrigerate for up to 1 week. Return to room
temperature before serving.

serving idea
Use as a sandwich spread for roast beef, turkey, or pulled pork,
or dollop atop beans or rice.

serve with beer
A light or dark Mexican beer, with lime

flatbread with feta, thyme, and oven-roasted tomatoes

I'm fortunate to have an outdoor wood-fired oven, and I use it to make flatbreads of all kinds, including this one inspired by ingredients from the Mediterranean. The feta adds a salty, slightly tart taste that balances the sweet, smoky flavors of the oven-roasted tomatoes.

1 package (2½ tsp)
active dry yeast

½ tsp sugar

2 Tbsp extra-virgin olive oil

2 cups (10 oz/315 g)
all-purpose flour,
or more as needed

1 tsp coarse sea salt

Cornmeal or rice flour
for dusting

FOR THE TOPPING

16 Oven-Roasted
Tomatoes (page 43)

3 tsp minced fresh thyme

6 oz (185 g) French feta
cheese, crumbled

20–24 oil-cured black olives,
pitted and halved

1 Tbsp extra-virgin olive oil

In a small bowl, dissolve the yeast in 1 cup (8 fl oz/250 ml) warm water (110°F/43°C), stir in the sugar, and let stand until foamy, about 5 minutes. Transfer the yeast mixture to a food processor. Add the olive oil, 2 cups flour, and salt and pulse until a soft dough forms, adding more flour if needed to reduce stickiness. Turn the dough out onto a lightly floured work surface and knead until smooth and elastic, about 7 minutes. Form into a ball, transfer to a lightly oiled bowl, turn to coat, and cover the bowl with a damp kitchen towel or plastic wrap. Let the dough rise in a warm, draft-free place until doubled in bulk, about 1 hour.

Place a baking stone in the oven and preheat to 500°F (260°C). Dust a rimless baking sheet with the cornmeal. Divide the dough in half. On a lightly floured work surface, roll out half of the dough into a rough oval about 12 inches (30 cm) long and ¼ inch (6 mm) thick. Transfer to the prepared baking sheet. Arrange half of the tomatoes evenly over the dough. Sprinkle evenly with half each of the thyme and cheese, and dot with half of the olives. Slide the flatbread onto the hot stone and bake until the crust is bubbly and crisp on the bottom, 10–15 minutes. Sprinkle with half of the oil, cut into pieces, and serve. Repeat with the remaining dough and toppings.

try different cheeses
Gorgonzola, soft goat cheese, fresh mozzarella, or Fontina

serve with wine
A light, fruity white such as Albariño or Pinot Grigio

crostini with herbed chèvre and kumquats

SERVES 6–8

This unusual combination of soft goat cheese, called chèvre, and kumquats is surprisingly pleasing. The slightly tangy goat cheese pairs wonderfully with the bright, juicy citrus fruit. Rubbing the crostini with garlic adds extra flavor, but you can omit it if you prefer.

1 baguette, cut on the diagonal into slices ¼ inch (6 mm) thick

2 Tbsp extra-virgin olive oil

3 cloves garlic, halved lengthwise

4–5 oz (125–155 g) chèvre (soft goat cheese), at room temperature

1 tsp minced fresh thyme, plus leaves for garnish (optional)

20–25 kumquats, about 1 lb (500 g) total weight, halved, seeded, and chopped

Preheat the oven to 350°F (180°C).

Lay the baguette slices on a rimmed baking sheet and brush the tops lightly with the olive oil. Bake until the undersides are lightly golden, about 6 minutes. Turn the slices and bake until lightly golden on the second side, about 5 minutes longer. Let cool, then rub the oiled side of the toasts with the cut sides of the garlic cloves.

In a bowl, using a fork, mash together the cheese and thyme.

Spread each toast with about 2 teaspoons of the herbed goat cheese and top with some of the chopped kumquats. Garnish with thyme leaves, if desired. Serve at once.

try different cheeses
Teleme or a smooth-spreading feta

serve with wine
A crisp, citrusy Sauvignon Blanc or Sancerre

spicy fromage blanc with garlic toasts

This is my version of a spread I first savored in Provence one fall, at a party to celebrate the grape harvest. The man who introduced me to it had made the *fromage blanc* from his own goat's milk, and it tasted divine. The *harissa* gives the creamy spread just a hint of fire.

1 baguette, cut on
the diagonal into slices
¼ inch (6 mm) thick

2 Tbsp extra-virgin olive oil

3 cloves garlic,
halved lengthwise

1 cup (8 oz/250 g)
fromage blanc

2 Tbsp heavy cream,
or as needed

2 Tbsp minced shallots

2 Tbsp minced fresh chives,
plus whole blades for
garnish

½ tsp sea salt

2 Tbsp *harissa,* or to taste

Preheat the oven to 350°F (180°C).

Lay the baguette slices on a rimmed baking sheet and brush the tops lightly with the olive oil. Bake until the undersides are lightly golden, about 6 minutes. Turn the slices and bake until lightly golden on the second side, about 5 minutes longer. Let cool, then rub the oiled side of the toasts with the cut sides of the garlic cloves.

In a bowl, mix together the *fromage blanc* and cream, adding a little more cream if needed to make a spreadable paste. Stir in the shallots, minced chives, salt, and *harissa*. Taste and adjust with more *harissa* if you want a spicier spread.

Spread the garlic toasts with the *fromage blanc* mixture. Arrange on a platter, garnish the platter with the chive blades, and serve at once.

try different cheeses
Boucheron or soft goat cheese

serve with wine
A crisp white such as Pinot Grigio, Sauvignon Blanc, or Sancerre

cheddar cheese crackers with mixed seeds

MAKES ABOUT
36 CRACKERS

Making your own crackers is fun and surprisingly easy. You can leave them plain or top them with seeds, spices, or chopped nuts. Cheddar, which has a strong yet smooth flavor and a semifirm texture, is my favorite cheese to use for crackers, biscuits, or muffins.

1½ cups (7½ oz/235 g) all-purpose flour, plus more for dusting

½ tsp coarse sea salt

⅛ tsp cayenne pepper

½ cup (4 oz/125 g) unsalted butter, at room temperature, cut into ½-inch (12-mm) pieces

2 cups (8 oz/250 g) shredded sharp Cheddar cheese

1 tsp caraway seeds

1 tsp white or black poppy seeds

1 tsp cumin seeds

Preheat the oven to 375°F (190°C). In a bowl, whisk together the flour, salt, and cayenne. In a food processor, combine the butter and cheese and process until a smooth paste forms. Add the flour mixture and pulse several times until a ragged dough forms. Remove the dough from the processor and shape it into a smooth ball.

To make rustic crackers, pinch off nuggets of the dough and shape between your palms into 1-inch (2.5-cm) balls. On a lightly floured work surface, roll out each ball into a round about ⅛ inch (3 mm) thick. To make more refined crackers, on a lightly floured surface, roll out the large dough ball into a sheet ⅛ inch thick. Using a pastry cutter about 1½ inches (4 cm) in diameter, cut out rounds. Gather up the dough scraps, reroll, and cut out more rounds.

Using a spatula, carefully transfer the dough rounds to one or more ungreased rimmed baking sheets, spacing them about ½ inch (12 mm) apart. In a small bowl, stir together the caraway, poppy, and cumin seeds. Scatter the mixed seeds evenly over the crackers, then gently press them into the dough. Bake until crisp and lightly golden, 12–15 minutes. Let cool for at least 10 minutes on the baking sheet(s) on a wire rack, then serve warm or at room temperature.

try different cheeses
A good melting cheese such as Monterey Jack or Swiss

serve with beer
Pilsner or IPA

pecorino and parmesan cheese straws

These slender straws feature two aged cheeses, one made from cow's milk and the other from sheep's milk. The Parmesan is milder, but its distinctive deep flavor is unmistakable; the rustic pecorino adds a salty sharpness. I often serve these straws to accompany soups and salads.

½ cup (4 oz/125 g) unsalted butter, at room temperature, cut into ½-inch (12-mm) pieces, plus more for greasing

5 oz (155 g) aged pecorino cheese, coarsely grated

5 oz (155 g) Parmesan cheese, preferably Parmigiano-Reggiano, coarsely grated

½ tsp freshly ground white pepper

¼ tsp cayenne pepper

1 cup (5 oz/155 g) all-purpose flour, plus more for dusting

In a food processor, combine the butter pieces, pecorino, Parmesan, and white and cayenne pepper and process until a smooth paste forms. Slowly add the flour while pulsing to blend. When all of the flour has been incorporated, remove the dough from the processor, shape into a smooth ball, wrap in plastic wrap, and refrigerate for at least 1 hour or up to 3 hours.

Preheat the oven to 350°F (180°C). Lightly butter a rimmed baking sheet, or line it with parchment paper. Cut the dough into 6 equal pieces. Work with 1 piece at a time and keep the others covered. On a lightly floured work surface, using the palms of your hands, roll the dough back and forth over the work surface until it is a narrow cylinder about the diameter of a drinking straw. Cut into 6- to 8-inch (15- to 20-cm) lengths. Place the lengths on the prepared baking sheet, spacing them about 2 inches (5 cm) apart. Repeat with the remaining dough pieces.

Bake the cheese straws until they are golden brown and lightly crisp, 15–20 minutes. Let cool for 5–10 minutes, then gently transfer to a serving platter and serve warm or at room temperature. Or, let cool completely, transfer to a loosely closed paper bag, and store in a dry place at room temperature for up to 5 days.

serve with wine or beer
Chianti, Sangiovese, or Barbera for red; Grüner Veltliner or Vermentino for white; or amber stout for beer

zucchini blossoms
stuffed with ricotta

The Italians are so fond of stuffed squash blossoms that they have developed zucchini varieties that produce large, strong blooms. I have such blossoms in my garden all summer. They can be stuffed with many different cheeses, but I adore the delicate taste of whole-milk ricotta.

18 large zucchini blossoms, stems intact

½ cup (4 oz/125 g) fresh whole-milk ricotta cheese

1½ cups (7½ oz/235 g) all-purpose flour

1 tsp fine sea salt

1 Tbsp extra-virgin olive oil

1 large egg, lightly beaten

Canola oil for frying

Fried fresh flat-leaf parsley sprigs for serving (optional)

Coarse sea salt for sprinkling

Remove the stamen from the center of each blossom. Gently wash and pat dry the blossoms. Spoon a heaping teaspoon of the ricotta into the center of each blossom. Twist the tips of the petals closed and set aside.

In a bowl, whisk together the flour and fine sea salt. Add the olive oil, egg, and 2 cups (16 fl oz/500 ml) water and whisk to make a batter.

Pour the canola oil into a deep sauté pan to a depth of 2 inches (5 cm). Heat over medium-high heat until it reaches 375°F (190°C) on a deep-frying thermometer. One at a time, gently slip the stuffed blossoms into the batter and turn to coat evenly. Using a slotted spatula, lift the blossoms from the batter, allowing the excess to drip off, and carefully lower into the hot oil. Fry in batches of 4 or 5, spacing them about 1 inch (2.5 cm) apart and turning once if needed to brown evenly, until golden brown, 1–2 minutes. Using the spatula, transfer to paper towels to drain.

If making the fried parsley garnish, when all of the blossoms are cooked, add the parsley sprigs to the hot oil and fry just until lightly crisped, about 30 seconds. Transfer to the paper towels to drain.

Sprinkle the zucchini blossoms with the coarse sea salt and top with the parsley, if desired. Serve at once.

try different cheeses
Soft goat cheese, feta, or fresh mozzarella

fried pecorino with stone-fruit salsa

When you heat aged pecorino in a frying pan, it crisps, rather than melting. (You can use the same technique with Parmesan cheese.) These crunchy wafers are delicate and delicious, and their saltiness is perfectly enhanced by a refreshing, chile-flecked summer-fruit salsa.

1 peach, halved, pitted, and finely chopped

2 nectarines, halved, pitted, and finely chopped

2 Tbsp thinly sliced red onion

¼ tsp red pepper flakes

2 Tbsp fresh lime juice

¼ tsp sea salt, or to taste

½ lb (250 g) pecorino cheese, cut into slices about ⅛ inch (3 mm) thick

To make the salsa, in a bowl, combine the peach, nectarines, red onion, and red pepper flakes. Add the lime juice and ¼ teaspoon salt and toss gently with a wooden spoon. Taste and adjust the seasoning with more salt, if needed. Set the salsa aside.

Heat a dry nonstick frying pan over medium heat. When it is hot, reduce the heat to low. Place the slices of cheese in the pan, being careful not to crowd the slices. When the edges of a slice are golden, flip it and cook the other side until the bottom is golden, 2–3 minutes longer, then transfer to a serving platter.

Serve the fried cheese slices at once, topped with the salsa.

try different cheeses
Parmigiano-Reggiano or *halloumi*

serve with wine
A sparkling wine or minerally white such as Sauvignon Blanc or Grüner Veltliner

grilled figs with dry jack and prosciutto

Grilling or roasting fresh figs gives them a caramelized, sweet flavor that enhances this classic Italian-style pairing of a salty cheese, cured meat, and ripe fruit. I like to serve the figs hot off the grill as a starter, or combine them with a simple arugula salad for a light meal.

16 soft fresh figs

2 Tbsp extra-virgin olive oil

3 oz (90 g) dry Jack cheese, thinly sliced

3 oz (90 g) prosciutto, thinly sliced, each slice cut in half or thirds to make 16 pieces

Preheat a grill to medium-high and oil the grill rack.

Arrange the figs in a single layer in a shallow baking dish. Drizzle with the olive oil and turn gently to coat them with the oil.

Place the figs on the hot grill and grill, turning once or twice, until the skins start to glisten and lightly char, about 3 minutes. (Alternatively, preheat the oven to 450°F/230°C. Place the figs, still in the shallow baking dish, in the oven and roast, turning several times, until shiny and plump, 5–7 minutes.)

Transfer the figs to a rack (or leave in the baking dish) until cool enough to handle. Slit each fig from the stem end almost to the bottom and slip a piece of cheese and a half-slice of prosciutto into the slit. Serve at once.

try different cheeses
Parmigiano-Reggiano or an aged pecorino

serve with wine
A full-bodied red such as Cabernet Sauvignon, Barbaresco, Côtes du Rhône, Languedoc, or Rioja

beaufort, chive, and black pepper gougères

I first saw Beaufort cheese being made in the French Alps, in the old province of Savoy, its place of origin. I tasted it at different stages of aging—nine months, one year, two years—and have been intrigued since. Its buttery flavor enhances these classic cheese puffs called *gougères*.

6 Tbsp (3 oz/90 g) unsalted butter

1 tsp sea salt

½ tsp freshly ground pepper

1 cup (5 oz/155 g) all-purpose flour

5 large eggs

1½ cups (6 oz/185 g) shredded Beaufort cheese

2 Tbsp minced fresh chives or fresh flat-leaf parsley

Preheat the oven to 425°F (220°C).

In a saucepan over medium-high heat, combine 1 cup (8 fl oz/250 ml) water and the butter, salt, and pepper. Bring to a boil, stirring constantly. Continue to cook until the butter has melted completely, 3–4 minutes. Add the flour all at once and mix vigorously with a wooden spoon until a thick paste forms and pulls away from the sides of the pan, about 3 minutes. Remove from the heat and make a well in the center. Crack 1 egg into the well and beat it, with the wooden spoon or a handheld mixer, into the hot mixture. Repeat with 3 more eggs, beating each egg into the hot mixture before adding the next egg; you should have 1 egg remaining. Add 1 cup (4 oz/125 g) of the cheese and the chives and mix well.

Line 2 rimmed baking sheets with parchment paper. To form each *gougère*, dip a teaspoon into cold water, then scoop up a generous teaspoon of the batter and push it onto the baking sheet with your fingertips. Repeat, dipping the spoon in the water each time to prevent sticking and spacing the mounds 3 inches (7.5 cm) apart. Lightly beat the remaining egg and brush the tops of the mounds with it, being careful none drips onto the pan, which can inhibit puffing. Sprinkle the tops evenly with the remaining ½ cup (2 oz/60 g) cheese.

Bake for 10 minutes, then reduce the heat to 350°F (180°C) and bake until golden and crunchy, about 15 minutes longer. Pierce each puff with a skewer to release the steam, turn off the oven, and leave the puffs in the oven for 10 minutes. Serve warm or at room temperature.

parmesan and black pepper popcorn

Popcorn is the simplest of snacks, but it reaches a new level of appeal when liberally sprinkled with cheese. Here, salty Parmesan meets earthy black pepper and mingles with a decadent combination of olive oil and butter to deliver maximum flavor.

2 Tbsp olive oil

½ cup (3 oz/90 g) popcorn kernels

1 Tbsp unsalted butter, melted

¼ cup (1 oz/30 g) freshly grated Parmesan cheese, preferably Parmigiano-Reggiano

Sea salt and freshly ground pepper

In a large saucepan over medium heat, warm 1 tablespoon of the olive oil. Add the kernels, cover the saucepan, and cook, shaking the pan often, until the popping slows, about 5 minutes. Remove from the heat and wait for the popping to subside before removing the lid.

Transfer the popcorn to a large bowl. Drizzle with the remaining 1 tablespoon olive oil and the melted butter, tossing to coat. Sprinkle with the Parmesan, season with salt and pepper, and toss again. Divide among individual bowls, if desired, and serve hot.

Cheddar and Rosemary Popcorn

Pop the popcorn as directed above, substituting canola oil for the olive oil. In a separate saucepan over low heat, whisk together 2 tablespoons unsalted butter and ¼ cup (1 oz/30 g) grated sharp Cheddar cheese just until the butter melts (the mixture may not be entirely smooth). Stir in 1 tablespoon minced fresh rosemary. Drizzle the mixture over the popcorn, toss to coat, and season with salt and pepper.

serve with wine or beer
A dry red such as Malbec, a crisp white such as Albariño, or any type of beer

soups & salads

A drawer in my refrigerator is devoted
to cheeses, and I always keep it well stocked. For salads,
which I make every night, I usually choose feta, Parmesan,
Crottin de Chavignol, fresh mozzarella, or a blue, which
I grate, shave, or crumble atop fresh-picked greens. For soups,
I typically reach for Cheddar, Gruyère, or fresh ricotta. I
also routinely save Parmesan rinds for tossing into pots of
simmering soup, where they both thicken the
broth and add a subtle, earthy flavor.

cheddar and ale soup with crispy shallots

This warming soup conjures English pub fare. The ale and seasonings add an aromatic and spicy tang that tempers the richness of the cheese. For the best flavor, use an extra-sharp Cheddar. Be careful not to let the soup boil once the cheese has been added, or it can cause the soup to be grainy.

¼ cup (2 fl oz/60 ml) canola oil

4–6 shallots, thinly sliced

2 yellow waxy potatoes

1 yellow onion

2 ribs celery

2 carrots, peeled

4 Tbsp (2 oz/60 g) unsalted butter

1 clove garlic, minced

⅓ cup (2 oz/60 g) all-purpose flour

1 tsp sea salt

½ tsp paprika

⅛ tsp cayenne pepper

2 cups (16 fl oz/500 ml) whole milk

½ cup (4 fl oz/125 ml) heavy cream

1½ cups (12 fl oz/375 ml) low-sodium chicken broth

1 bottle (12 fl oz/375 ml) ale

1 Tbsp Worcestershire sauce

1 tsp dry mustard

1 lb (500 g) Cheddar cheese, shredded

In a frying pan over medium-high heat, warm the canola oil. Add the shallots and cook, turning once or twice, until crisp and golden, about 5 minutes. Using a slotted spoon, transfer to a bowl and set aside.

Cut the potatoes into ½-inch (12-mm) cubes; chop the onion, celery, and carrots. In a saucepan over medium-high heat, melt the butter. Add the potatoes, onion, celery, carrots, and garlic, reduce the heat to medium-low, and cook, stirring, until the onion, celery, and carrots have softened and the potatoes are almost tender, 7–10 minutes. Sprinkle the vegetables with the flour, salt, paprika, and cayenne and stir until the flour is lightly browned. Slowly add the milk, scraping up any bits clinging to the bottom of the pan. Pour in the cream, broth, ale, Worcestershire sauce, and mustard, whisking constantly. Raise the heat to medium and continue to cook, stirring, to allow the flavors to blend, about 5 minutes; be careful not to let the mixture boil. Add in the cheese and cook, stirring, until the cheese has just melted, 2–3 minutes.

Remove from the heat and purée with an immersion blender or purée in batches in a regular blender. Reheat just until steaming. Ladle into warmed bowls, garnish with the crispy shallots, and serve at once.

serve with wine or beer
A full-bodied red, crisp white, brown ale, or hoppy IPA

soups & salads   91

onion soup gratinée

SERVES 6–8

My daughter, her soon-to-be French mother-in-law, and I made this soup two days before my daughter's wedding, which was held at my home. Her vision was to serve French onion soup at midnight, and we did, inviting the band and all remaining guests to join us.

6 Tbsp (3 oz/90 g) unsalted butter

1 Tbsp extra-virgin olive oil

2 lb (1 kg) yellow onions, very thinly sliced

½ tsp sugar

½ tsp sea salt

1½ tsp all-purpose flour

8 cups (64 fl oz/2 l) low-sodium beef broth

1 cup (8 fl oz/250 ml) dry white wine

1 tsp freshly ground pepper

FOR THE TOPPING

12–16 slices coarse country bread, each ½ inch (12 mm) thick

2 cloves garlic, halved lengthwise

3 Tbsp extra-virgin olive oil

2 cups (8 oz/250 g) shredded Gruyère or Emmentaler cheese

2 Tbsp unsalted butter, cut into small pieces

In a heavy saucepan over medium heat, melt the butter with the olive oil. Add the onions and cook, stirring, until translucent, 4–5 minutes. Reduce the heat to low, cover, and cook until lightly golden, about 10 minutes. Uncover, sprinkle with the sugar and salt, and raise the heat to medium. Cook, stirring often, until the onions are golden brown, 20–30 minutes.

Sprinkle the flour over the onions and stir until the flour is browned, 2–3 minutes. Slowly add the broth and 2 cups (16 fl oz/500 ml) water, stirring constantly. Raise the heat to high and bring to a boil. Stir in the wine and pepper, reduce the heat to low, cover, and cook until the onions begin to break down, about 45 minutes.

Meanwhile, ready the topping. Preheat the broiler. Put the bread slices on a baking sheet and broil, turning once, until dry but not colored, about 3 minutes per side. Rub both sides of each slice with the cut sides of the garlic cloves, then brush both sides with the olive oil. Return to the broiler and broil, turning once, until lightly golden, about 2 minutes per side.

Preheat the oven to 450°F (230°C). Place 6–8 ovenproof bowls on a rimmed baking sheet. Ladle in the soup, top each bowl with 2 toasted bread slices, top the bread with the cheese, and then dot with the butter. Bake until a golden crust forms on top and the soup bubbles at the edges, about 15 minutes. Serve at once.

serve with wine
A medium-bodied red such as Barbera or Côtes du Rhône

parmesan, leek, and chickpea soup

SERVES 4–6

Don't let this soup's light appearance fool you. It's rich with flavor, and a classic Italian favorite. Chickpeas and leeks add heft and texture, and the Parmesan cheese lends a saltiness. For a thicker version, remove 1 cup (8 fl oz/250 ml) of the soup base, purée it, then stir it back into the soup.

6 cups (48 fl oz/1.5 l) low-sodium chicken broth or beef broth

3 Tbsp dry white wine

3–4 large leeks, white and pale green parts only, sliced

1–1½-oz (30–45-g) piece Parmesan cheese rind, preferably Parmigiano-Reggiano

1 can (15 oz/470 g) chickpeas, drained and rinsed

Sea salt and freshly ground pepper

⅓ cup (1½ oz/45 g) freshly grated Parmesan cheese, preferably Parmigiano-Reggiano, for sprinkling

In a saucepan over high heat, combine the broth and wine and bring to a boil. Cook until reduced by 1–2 tablespoons, about 2 minutes. Add the leeks and the cheese rind and reduce the heat to low. Cover and simmer until the leeks are translucent, the rind has melted a bit, and the broth is nicely flavored by both the cheese and the leeks, about 25 minutes.

Add the chickpeas and continue to cook until they are heated through, about 5 minutes. Remove and discard the cheese rind. Season with salt and pepper to taste.

Ladle the soup into warmed bowls and serve at once. Pass the grated cheese at the table for sprinkling.

serve with wine
An Italian red such as Sangiovese, Chianti, or a varietal from the Piedmont region

basil soup with fromage blanc and tomatoes

Traditionally made from cow's milk, *fromage blanc* is a soft, fresh cheese with a sweet-sour flavor. The French sometimes sprinkle it with sugar for dessert, but it can also be used as a base for spreads, stirred into pan juices to make a sauce, or used to thicken and flavor soups, as done here.

4 bunches fresh basil, about 3 oz (90 g) total weight

1 Tbsp unsalted butter

¼ cup (1½ oz/45 g) minced shallots

½ lb (250 g) potatoes, peeled and cut into small cubes

4 cups (32 fl oz/1 l) low-sodium chicken broth

3 Tbsp *fromage blanc*

Juice of 1 lemon

Sea salt and freshly ground pepper

12–15 cherry tomatoes, halved or quartered

Remove the leaves from the basil stems, reserving about 40 of the smallest leaves for garnish. Coarsely chop the remaining basil leaves and set aside.

In a saucepan, melt the butter over medium heat. Add the shallots and sauté until limp, 2–3 minutes. Add the potatoes and stir several times. Add the chopped basil and the broth, reduce the heat to low, cover, and cook until the potatoes are tender, about 15 minutes. Purée the soup with an immersion blender or in batches in a regular blender. Reheat just until steaming, then stir in the *fromage blanc* and lemon juice. Season with salt and pepper.

Ladle the soup into warmed bowls, and garnish with the reserved basil leaves and the tomatoes. Serve at once.

serve with wine
A light, fruity, high-acid white such as Pinot Grigio, Riesling, or Albariño

radicchio and endive with aged gouda and red-wine vinaigrette

SERVES 4–6

Aged Gouda is a dense, golden-hued cheese with bits of crunchy milk solids that complement the crisp, pleasantly bitter red radicchio and endive in this winter salad. You can either cut the Gouda into small squares or use a vegetable peeler to create more delicate shavings.

FOR THE VINAIGRETTE

2 Tbsp balsamic vinegar

¼ cup (2 fl oz/60 ml) dry red wine such as Merlot or Syrah

½ tsp sea salt

¼ cup (2 fl oz/60 ml) extra-virgin olive oil

4 heads Belgian endive, red if possible

½ head radicchio, torn into bite-sized pieces

½ cup (½ oz/15 g) fresh flat-leaf parsley leaves

¼ lb (125 g) aged Gouda, shaved or coarsely chopped

Freshly ground pepper

To make the vinaigrette, in a small saucepan over medium-low heat, combine the vinegar and wine and bring to a simmer. Cook until reduced by half, about 3 minutes. Set aside to cool. In the bottom of a large bowl, using a fork, mix together the salt, the reduced vinegar and wine mixture, and the olive oil just to blend. Set aside.

Cut each endive in half lengthwise, and cut away the solid cone-shaped base. Roughly chop the leaves, cut them lengthwise into strips, or leave them whole if small. Add the radicchio, parsley, and endive to the bowl with the vinaigrette and toss well.

Divide the salad among 4–6 plates. Top each with an equal amount of the cheese and a sprinkle of pepper. Serve at once.

try different cheeses
A sharp, semifirm cheese such as Parmigiano-Reggiano, aged Gruyère, or Manchego

serve with wine
A rich white such as Chardonnay or Viognier or medium-bodied red like Grenache or Beaujolais

crottin salad with pears, fennel, and currants

My French son-in-law brings me cheese from France, and I especially love it when it's Crottin de Chavignol. It keeps for weeks, getting harder and more flavorful as it ages. When it is well aged, I often grate it into vinaigrettes or salads, where even a bit brings the taste of France to a dish.

2 bulbs fennel

1 Tbsp sherry vinegar

3 Tbsp extra-virgin olive oil

1 aged Crottin de Chavignol or other small, round aged goat cheese, about 2 oz (60 g), coarsely grated

½ tsp sea salt or kosher salt

¼ tsp freshly ground white pepper

1½ cups (1½ oz/45 g) mâche or baby arugula

3 pears, halved, cored, and thinly sliced

⅓ cup (2 oz/60 g) dried currants

Cut the stems and feathery leaves from each fennel bulb. Reserve a few of the leaves for garnish and discard the remainder and the stems. Trim off the base from each bulb. If the outer layer of either bulb is tough or discolored, discard it. Using a mandoline, or a very sharp chef's knife, cut each bulb lengthwise into paper-thin slices. Then, using a knife, cut each slice lengthwise into strips ¼ inch (6 mm) wide.

In a large bowl, using a fork, mix together the vinegar, olive oil, 1 tablespoon of the grated cheese, and the salt and pepper. Add the fennel and toss to coat well. Divide the mâche among 4–6 plates. Top with some of the dressed fennel, then add the sliced pears and a sprinkle of currants. Sprinkle with the remaining cheese and garnish with a few fennel leaves. Serve at once.

try different cheeses
Any aged goat's milk cheese such as Selles-sur-Cher
or Redwood Hill's California Crottin

serve with wine
A crisp, minerally white wine such as Sancerre,
Pouilly-Fumé, or Sauvignon Blanc

grilled romaine and halloumi with mint vinaigrette

Halloumi, a stretched curd cheese traditionally made from a mixture of sheep's and goat's milk, originated in Cypress and is now wildly popular all over the Middle East. When grilled or fried, it melts and softens but retains a firm structure, ideal for a starter or salad.

FOR THE VINAIGRETTE

¼ tsp sea salt or to taste

2 Tbsp red wine vinegar

3 Tbsp extra-virgin olive oil

¼ cup (⅓ oz/10 g) minced fresh mint

¼ tsp freshly ground black pepper

¼ tsp red pepper flakes

2 heads romaine lettuce, quartered lengthwise

½ lb (250 g) *halloumi* cheese, cut into slices ⅓ inch (9 mm) thick

2 Tbsp extra-virgin olive oil

Preheat a grill to medium-high and oil the grill rack.

To make the vinaigrette, in a bowl, whisk together the ¼ tsp salt, vinegar, and olive oil. Stir in the mint, black pepper, and red pepper flakes. Taste and adjust the seasoning with salt, if needed. Set aside.

Place the romaine quarters and *halloumi* slices on a baking sheet and brush with the olive oil. Place the romaine, cut side down, on the grill rack and grill until seared and the edges of the leaves are golden, about 5 minutes. Turn and grill the other side until almost limp, 3–4 minutes longer. Transfer to a platter, cut side up. Place the *halloumi* slices on the grill and grill until the edges soften, the interior is warm, and golden grill marks appear, about 2 minutes. Turn and grill on the second side for 1–2 minutes longer, until lightly golden. Add the *halloumi* to the platter with the grilled romaine.

Pour the vinaigrette over the warm salad and serve at once.

try different cheeses
Fresh mozzarella, pecorino, or feta

serve with wine
A dry rosé or sparkling wine

shaved fennel, parmesan, and arugula salad

I first had a version of this salad while traveling near Ravenna, Italy. Previously, I'd only enjoyed fennel cooked. The thinly shaved, faintly anise-flavored vegetable is transformed when served with a rich olive oil vinaigrette, peppery arugula, and a pile of fresh Parmesan shavings.

2 bulbs fennel

3 Tbsp extra-virgin olive oil

1½ tsp fresh lemon juice, or as needed

1 tsp Champagne vinegar

½ tsp sea salt

½ tsp freshly ground pepper

4 cups (4 oz/125 g) baby arugula leaves

2-oz (60-g) piece Parmesan cheese, preferably Parmigiano-Reggiano

Cut the stems and feathery leaves from each fennel bulb. Reserve a few of the leaves for garnish and discard the remainder and the stems. Trim off the base from each bulb. If the outer layer of either bulb is tough or discolored, discard it. Using a mandoline, or a very sharp chef's knife, cut each bulb lengthwise into paper-thin slices. Then, using a knife, cut each slice lengthwise into several pieces.

In a large bowl, using a fork, mix together the olive oil, lemon juice, vinegar, salt, and pepper. Taste and add more lemon juice, if desired. Add the fennel and toss to coat well. Let stand for 10–15 minutes, then add the arugula and toss to coat well.

Divide the salad among 4–6 plates. Using a vegetable peeler, shave the cheese into thin slices or curls, and divide among the salads. Garnish with a few fennel leaves. Serve at once.

try different cheeses
Grana padano or an aged sheep's milk cheese like *pecorino romano*

serve with wine
A full-bodied red such as Sangiovese, Chianti, or Côtes du Rhône

roasted beets with ricotta salata and wild arugula

Wild arugula has more intense peppery flavor than cultivated arugula and smaller, darker leaves. Combine it with roasted beets, a light vinaigrette, and slivers of dry, salty ricotta salata—a fantastic topping for salads and soups—for a rustic dish worthy of an Italian farmhouse.

3 beets, any color, about 1 lb (470 g) total weight

4 Tbsp (2 fl oz/60 ml) extra-virgin olive oil

2 Tbsp fresh orange juice

1 Tbsp fresh lemon juice

¼ tsp Dijon mustard

½ tsp sea salt

¼ tsp freshly ground white pepper

2 cups (2 oz/60 g) wild arugula, tough stems removed

4–5 oz (125–155 g) *ricotta salata* cheese, thinly sliced

Preheat the oven to 350°F (180°C).

If still attached, trim off the greens from the beets, leaving 1 inch (2.5 cm) of the stem intact. Rub the beets with 1½ tablespoons of the olive oil. Put the beets in a small roasting pan and roast, turning once or twice, until tender when pierced with a fork, 1–1¼ hours. Remove from the oven and let cool. Peel the beets, cut them into thin slices, and set aside.

In a salad bowl, using a fork, mix together the orange and lemon juices, the remaining 2½ tablespoons olive oil, the mustard, and the salt and pepper. Add the sliced beets to the bowl and turn gently to coat well with the dressing. Add the arugula and toss until well mixed.

Divide the beet and arugula mixture among 4 plates. Top each salad with some of the *ricotta salata* and serve at once.

try different cheeses
A good-quality feta made from goat's milk, sheep's milk, or cow's milk, or a mixture

serve with wine
A spicy Zinfandel for red or dry Riesling for white

warm squash salad with teleme and pepitas

The extra step of both steaming and roasting the squash brings a caramelized taste to this autumnal salad. The oven-hot squash warms the spinach and melts the edges of the tart, semisoft Teleme, blending the flavors. Sometimes I substitute walnuts or hazelnuts for the *pepitas*.

1 small butternut squash, about 1½ lb (750 g)

2 Tbsp extra-virgin olive oil, plus more for drizzling

Sea salt and freshly ground pepper

2 tsp white balsamic vinegar

1 tsp sherry vinegar

2 Tbsp walnut oil or hazelnut oil

4 cups (4 oz/125 g) baby spinach leaves

¼ lb (125 g) Teleme cheese, cut into ½-inch (12-mm) pieces

¼ cup (1 oz/30 g) *pepitas* (shelled pumpkin seeds)

Using a vegetable peeler, peel the squash. Cut it in half lengthwise, then scoop out and discard the seeds and fibers. Cut the squash into small slices or ½-inch (12-mm) cubes. Bring water to a boil in a steamer pan. Arrange the squash pieces on the steamer rack, place over the boiling water, cover, and steam until just slightly tender when pierced with a fork, 8–10 minutes. Remove the squash from the steamer and let cool.

Preheat the oven to 400°F (200°C). Line a rimmed baking sheet with parchment paper. Place the squash pieces on the baking sheet. Drizzle generously with olive oil and sprinkle with salt and pepper. Turn to coat. Roast, turning once, until lightly golden, 10–12 minutes.

In a large salad bowl, using a fork, mix together the vinegars, the 2 tablespoons olive oil, the walnut oil, ½ teaspoon salt, and ¼ teaspoon pepper. Add the spinach and toss to coat well.

Divide the spinach equally among 4–6 plates. Top with the warm squash pieces, the cheese, and a sprinkling of *pepitas*. Serve at once.

try different cheeses
Buffalo mozzarella, Fontina, or a creamy Monterey Jack

serve with wine or beer
A Chardonnay, Chenin Blanc, or stout

butter lettuce with sheep's milk cheese and hazelnuts

SERVES 4–6

The Pyrenees region in southwestern France is noted for its raw sheep's milk cheeses, most of which are aged, dry, and salty—just right for this delicate, delicious salad. I like creamy, tart-rinded Ossau-Iraty, which contrasts well with the sweet honey and crunchy nuts.

¾ cup (4 oz/125 g) hazelnuts

1 large or 2 medium heads butter lettuce

3 Tbsp extra-virgin olive oil

1 Tbsp white balsamic vinegar

I Tbsp Champagne vinegar

2 tsp honey

½ tsp sea salt

¼ lb (125 g) aged sheep's milk cheese, crumbled

In a dry frying pan over medium-low heat, toast the hazelnuts, stirring, until fragrant, about 5 minutes. Let cool, chop coarsely, and set aside.

Separate the leaves from the head(s) of lettuce. Tear the larger leaves into several pieces, but keep the medium and small leaves whole. You should have 4–5 cups (4–5 oz/125–155 g).

In a large salad bowl, using a fork, mix together the olive oil, vinegars, honey, and salt. Add the lettuce leaves and toss to coat well. Add half of the cheese and half of the hazelnuts and toss well. Top with the remaining cheese and nuts. Serve at once.

try different cheeses
An aged pecorino or Manchego, or an aged goat cheese

serve with wine
Malbec, Bordeaux, or Côtes du Rhône for red, or a crisp dry rosé

greens with artisanal cheeses and charcuterie

For this dish, I combined two classic French courses that I adore, charcuterie and cheese. The result is a riff on a chef's salad, which I enjoy serving antipasto style. Every time I make it, I pick a different mix of local cheeses to feature along with a selection of meats.

3 Tbsp extra-virgin olive oil

1 Tbsp red wine vinegar

¼ tsp sea salt

Freshly ground pepper

3 cups (3 oz/90 g) packed mixed baby greens such as wild arugula or mâche, tough stems removed

½ lb (250 g) prosciutto, serrano ham, or *coppa*, sliced paper-thin

1–2 *saucisson sec* or salami, whole or thinly sliced

3 oz (90 g) sheep's milk cheese, cut into wedges

3 oz (90 g) aged goat's milk cheese, cut into wedges

3 oz (90 g) cow's milk cheese, cut into wedges

In a large bowl, using a fork, mix together the olive oil, vinegar, and salt. Season to taste with pepper. Add the greens and toss lightly.

Arrange the dressed greens on one side of a serving platter. On the same platter (or on an additional plate or cutting board), arrange the meats and cheeses. Serve at once.

serve with wine

A full-bodied red such as Rioja or Merlot or lush white like Grüner Veltliner or Pinot Blanc

shaved zucchini salad with pecorino and almonds

SERVES 4–6

Aged pecorino is transformed into airy curls with the swipe of a vegetable peeler. Here the cheese, along with toasted almonds, adds beauty and flavor to a delicate arugula salad that stars summer-fresh zucchini cut into matchsticks and a light balsamic vinaigrette.

3 Tbsp extra-virgin olive oil

1 Tbsp balsamic vinegar

1 tsp red wine vinegar

½ tsp sea salt

½ tsp freshly ground pepper

2 small zucchini, about
4 inches (10 cm) long and
1 inch (2.5 cm) in diameter

2 cups (2 oz/60 g)
packed baby arugula

2 oz (60 g) pecorino cheese

½ cup (2½ oz/75 g)
almonds, toasted
and coarsely chopped

In a large bowl, using a fork, mix together the olive oil, vinegars, and salt and pepper to make a vinaigrette. Set aside.

Using a mandoline, slice the zucchini lengthwise into matchsticks. Or, using a very sharp chef's knife, cut the zucchini lengthwise into very thin slices, then cut the slices into matchsticks. Pat the zucchini dry on paper towels (excess moisture will dilute the vinaigrette).

Combine the arugula and zucchini in a large bowl and toss with the vinaigrette to coat well. Divide the salad among 4–6 plates or bowls. Using a vegetable peeler, shave the pecorino into thin curls and divide among the salads. Scatter the almonds over the top and serve at once.

try different cheeses
Parmigiano-Reggiano, *grana padano,*
or an aged goat cheese

serve with wine
A bright New Zealand Sauvignon Blanc
or light-bodied red such as Beaujolais

watermelon, feta, and mint salad with lime

SERVES 4

When I serve any version of this simple salad, there are never leftovers; even children devour it. I grow a few watermelon plants every year and prefer the small, seedless red and yellow varieties. Here, the tangy feta, lime juice, and fresh mint elevate the flavor of the lush fruit.

1 seedless watermelon, 2–4 lb (1–2 kg)

¼ cup (⅓ oz/10 g) chopped fresh mint, plus small leaves for garnish

Juice of 4 limes (about ½ cup/4 fl oz/125 ml)

¼ lb (125 g) feta cheese, crumbled

Lime zest for garnish

Halve the watermelon, then cut each half into 2–3 wedges. Cut the flesh away from the rind, then cut the flesh into wedges, slices, or 1-inch (2.5-cm) cubes. Put the watermelon in a bowl, sprinkle with the chopped mint, and pour the lime juice over. Turn several times to coat the melon evenly with the lime juice. Add half of the cheese and turn again.

Transfer to a serving platter, individual salad plates, or bowls. Garnish with the remaining feta, the mint leaves, and the lime zest and serve at once.

try a different cheese
A young, fresh goat cheese

serve with wine or beer
A jammy Beaujolais, dry Fumé Blanc, or cold pilsner

waldorf salad
with blue cheese

SERVES 4–6

A wide selection of both domestic and imported blue cheeses is available these days, and they vary in texture and taste. For this salad, a modern riff on a classic, I like to use a blue cheese that is dry and crumbly, such as Cabrales or Valdeón, but a creamy Gorgonzola would also work.

3 Tbsp extra-virgin olive oil

2 tsp Champagne vinegar or white wine vinegar

3 oz (90 g) blue cheese

2 Tbsp minced shallots

¼ tsp freshly ground pepper

6 heads Belgian endive, white or red

2 sweet, tart apples such as Gala, Honeycrisp, or Fuji, halved, cored, and sliced paper-thin

½ cup (2 oz/60 g) chopped walnuts, toasted (page 40)

2 Tbsp snipped fresh chives (about ¾-inch/2-cm lengths)

In a large bowl, combine the olive oil, vinegar, and one-third of the cheese. Using a fork, mash in the cheese to create a vinaigrette. Stir in the shallots and pepper. Set aside.

You can quarter, slice, or chop the endives. If quartering, cut away most of the solid cone-shaped base from each endive, leaving only enough to hold each quarter together, then cut the endives lengthwise into quarters. Or, cut away the entire base and thinly slice or coarsely chop the leaves.

In a large bowl, combine the endive and apples and toss gently to mix. Divide among 4–6 plates. Crumble the remaining two-thirds of the cheese over the top, dividing it evenly, then pour the vinaigrette over the salads. Sprinkle with the walnuts and the chives. Serve at once.

serve with wine
A sparkling wine such as prosecco or *cava*, or Sauvignon Blanc, Chenin Blanc, or dry rosé

mains

Cheese is a common addition to many
main dishes I regularly cook, such as pastas,
enchiladas, and roasted chicken, to name a few. As it
melts and binds with the other ingredients, it delivers
a wealth of flavor and complexity. I also like to vary
some favorite dishes by changing the cheese, such as
trading out a velvety Gorgonzola for a sharp Cheddar in
macaroni and cheese, or a nutty Fontina for a mildly
pungent Taleggio in a creamy risotto.

cheese fondue

I am so glad that cheese fondue has once again become fashionable. Paired with a simple green salad and crisp white wine, it makes a convivial winter meal. Here, the combination of piquant Emmentaler with stronger, creamier Gruyère yields a fondue that's rich and flavorful.

6 cloves garlic

2 cups (16 fl oz/500 ml) dry white wine such as Sauvignon Blanc

1¾ lb (875 g) Gruyère cheese, shredded

¾ lb (375 g) Emmentaler cheese, shredded

2 Tbsp kirsch

1 tsp freshly grated nutmeg

½ tsp freshly ground white pepper

1½ day-old baguettes or equivalent amount of artisanal nut, herb, or whole-grain bread, cut into ½-inch (12-mm) cubes

If using a ceramic fondue pot, set the oven to 250°F (120°C) and put the fondue pot in the oven to warm. If using a metal fondue pot, skip this step. Fill the burner of the fondue pot with denatured alcohol.

Crush the garlic with a garlic press or grate with a grater and put into a large, heavy-bottomed saucepan or directly into the metal fondue pot. Add the wine and place the pan over high heat. As soon as bubbles form around the edges, after about 2 minutes, reduce the heat to medium-low and add the cheeses, a little at a time, stirring with a wooden spoon. Continue to cook, stirring constantly, until the cheese melts completely into a smooth, creamy mass. Stir in the kirsch, nutmeg, and pepper.

To serve, light the burner of the fondue pot and place it on the table. Pour the hot fondue from the saucepan into the warmed ceramic pot, or transfer the metal fondue pot directly to the burner. Set out fondue forks and pass the bread cubes.

try different cheeses
Use an equal amount of grated Beaufort for the Gruyère. Use an equal amount of mild, soft blue such as Blue Castello or Montbriac, raclette, or a triple cream such as Brillat-Savarin for the Emmentaler.

serve with wine
Pinot Grigio, Sauvignon Blanc, or an Alsatian Gewürztraminer for white or Brunello, Pinot Noir, or Burgundy for red

risotto with taleggio, radicchio, and red wine

In this refined risotto, the seared radicchio, which tastes slightly bitter, is balanced by the creamy Taleggio, a washed-rind cow's milk cheese with a strong aroma but mild flavor. It melts readily, making it a good option to stir into risotto or polenta. Gently swirl in the cheese just before serving.

1 Tbsp extra-virgin olive oil

2 cups (6 oz/185 g) shredded radicchio (about 1 small head)

2 cups (16 fl oz/500 ml) low-sodium chicken broth

2 cups (16 fl oz/500 ml) low-sodium beef broth

2 Tbsp unsalted butter

½ yellow onion, finely chopped

2 cups (14 oz/440 g) Arborio rice

2 cups (16 fl oz/500 ml) dry red wine such as Pinot Noir or Merlot

6 oz (185 g) Taleggio cheese, rind removed and cut into small pieces

Sea salt and freshly ground pepper

⅓ cup (1½ oz/45 g) walnuts, toasted and chopped (optional)

Chopped fresh flat-leaf parsley for garnish (optional)

In a frying pan over medium-high heat, warm the olive oil. When it is hot, add the radicchio and sauté, stirring often, until the edges are golden, about 4 minutes. Transfer to paper towels to drain. In a saucepan over medium heat, combine the chicken and beef broths and bring to a simmer. Reduce the heat so the broth mixture barely simmers.

In another saucepan over medium-high heat, melt 1 tablespoon of the butter. When it foams, add the onion and cook until translucent, about 2 minutes. Add the rice and stir until it becomes opaque, about 2 minutes. Add the wine, a little at a time, and cook, stirring constantly, until all of the wine is nearly absorbed, 5–6 minutes. Reduce the heat to medium, add a ladleful of the hot broth mixture, and cook, stirring constantly, until the liquid is almost fully absorbed. Continue adding the broth, a ladleful at a time and stirring constantly, until the rice is tender but still slightly firm in the center and creamy, about 20 minutes.

Stir in the radicchio, the remaining 1 tablespoon butter, and the cheese and season with salt and pepper. Spoon into warmed bowls, top with the walnuts and parsley, if desired, and serve at once.

serve with wine
A medium-bodied red such as Chianti, Sangiovese, or Sagrantino

raclette

The first time I had raclette was in a chalet high in the French Alps. We ate in front of the fireplace. The cheese was set next to the fire, and as it melted, we took turns scraping the hot cheese onto our boiled potatoes. We sipped a lush, local wine. It was a simple yet unforgettable meal.

12 small to medium boiling potatoes such as Yukon gold, Yellow Finn, or White Rose

1 tsp sea salt

1–1½ lb (500–750 g) raclette cheese

Cornichons for serving

Coarse country bread, thinly sliced, for serving

Freshly ground pepper

In a large saucepan over medium-high heat, combine the potatoes, salt, and water to cover. Bring to a boil, reduce the heat to medium, and cook, uncovered, until the potatoes are easily pierced with the tip of a sharp knife, 20–25 minutes. Drain and cover to keep warm.

Preheat the oven to 400°F (200°C). Cut the raclette into slices about ½ inch (12 mm) thick and remove the rind. Arrange the slices on 4 individual ovenproof plates. Place the plates in the oven and cook until the cheese is melted, 5–7 minutes.

Meanwhile, transfer the potatoes to a serving bowl and arrange the cornichons and bread slices on a platter. Remove the plates of melted cheese from the oven, sprinkle with pepper, and serve at once, along with the potatoes, cornichons, and bread for dipping.

serve with wine
A rich white such as unoaked Chardonnay, Grüner Veltliner, Viognier, Vouvray, or white Burgundy

penne with ricotta salata, grilled zucchini, and onions

SERVES 4–6

When summer's first zucchini arrive in my garden, I cook them every way I can think of. *Ricotta salata* is a pressed and aged ricotta cheese similar to feta but less salty. In this pasta dish, it's the perfect foil for the sweetness of the caramelized onions and the charred flavor of the zucchini.

2 zucchini, cut into slices ¼ inch (6 mm) thick

4 Tbsp (2 fl oz/60 ml) extra-virgin olive oil

1 Tbsp chopped fresh oregano

Sea salt and freshly ground pepper

1 Tbsp unsalted butter

1 yellow onion, halved and thinly sliced crosswise

¾ lb (375 g) penne or other small pasta

¼ lb (125 g) *ricotta salata* cheese, shaved with a vegetable peeler

In a bowl, combine the zucchini, 1 tablespoon of the olive oil, the oregano, ½ teaspoon salt, and pepper to taste. Toss to coat well. Set the zucchini aside.

Preheat a grill to medium-high and oil the grill rack. Arrange the zucchini in a grill basket and grill, turning several times, until golden on both sides, 10–12 minutes. Set aside.

In a frying pan over medium-high heat, melt the butter with 1 tablespoon of the olive oil. When the butter foams, add the onion and reduce the heat to medium. Sprinkle with salt and cook, stirring occasionally, until the onion turns mahogany in color, 15–20 minutes. Keep warm.

Bring a large pot of salted water to a boil over high heat. Add the penne, stir well, and cook until the pasta is al dente, according to package directions.

Drain the pasta and transfer to a warmed serving bowl. Add the onion and any pan juices, the grilled zucchini, the remaining 2 tablespoons olive oil, and one-half of the cheese. Toss well. Sprinkle with the remaining cheese and serve at once.

serve with wine
A light, fruity white such as Pinot Grigio, Albariño, or Sauvignon Blanc

macaroni with farmhouse cheddar and bacon

Here's a seriously grown-up version of a kid's classic. Thanks to their different ages, the two Cheddars give this hearty baked pasta a richness that's balanced by the addition of salty, smoky bacon. A scattering of toasted coarse bread crumbs provides a crunchy, crusty top layer.

4 Tbsp (2 oz/60 g) unsalted butter, plus more for greasing

4 slices baguette or other firm bread, crusts removed and torn into bread crumbs

4 slices thick-cut bacon, cut crosswise into pieces ½ inch (12 mm) wide

¼ cup (1½ oz/45 g) flour

Salt and freshly ground black pepper

¼ tsp cayenne pepper

3 cups (24 fl oz/750 ml) whole milk, heated

½ lb (250 g) farmstead Cheddar cheese, shredded

¼ lb (125 g) white Cheddar cheese, coarsely grated

½ lb (250 g) elbow macaroni

Butter a shallow 1½-quart (48–fl oz/1.5-l) baking dish. In a small frying pan over medium-high, melt 1 tablespoon of the butter. Add the bread crumbs and fry until golden, about 4 minutes. Drain on paper towels.

In a frying pan over medium heat, fry the bacon until cooked but not crisp, 3–5 minutes. Drain on paper towels. In a saucepan over medium-high heat, melt the remaining 3 tablespoons butter. When the butter foams, whisk in the flour, ½ teaspoon salt, ¼ teaspoon black pepper, and the cayenne until a paste forms. Slowly whisk in the hot milk, reduce the heat to medium, and cook, whisking constantly, until thickened, about 15 minutes. Add three-fourths of the farmstead Cheddar and half of the white Cheddar and stir until melted, 1–2 minutes. Remove from the heat.

Preheat the oven to 375°F (190°C). Bring a large pot of salted water to a boil over high heat. Add the macaroni, stir well, and cook until the pasta is al dente, according to package directions. Drain, add to the prepared baking dish, and toss with the bacon. Pour in the cheese sauce and toss to mix well. Top with all the remaining cheese and then the bread crumbs. Bake until the sauce is bubbling and the top is golden, about 30 minutes. Let stand for a few minutes before serving.

serve with wine
A full-bodied red such as Merlot, Zinfandel, or Syrah

agnolini with goat cheese, fresh ricotta, peas, and herbs

SERVES 4–6

Agnolini, like ravioli, are filled pasta. These half-moons, made by cutting the pasta into circles and then folding them in half, are a perfect pocket for cheese. Ricotta is the traditional filling, but goat cheese adds a tang and complements spring peas and herbs. Serve with a crisp white wine.

FOR THE FILLING

1½ tsp extra-virgin olive oil

1 Tbsp finely chopped onion

¼ cup (1½ oz/45 g) frozen petite peas

¼ cup (2 oz/60 g) fresh whole-milk ricotta cheese

3 oz (90 g) soft goat cheese

1 egg

2 Tbsp chopped fresh chives

1 Tbsp chopped fresh mint, plus fresh mint leaves for garnish (optional)

½ tsp sea salt

All-purpose flour for dusting

12 oz (375 g) purchased fresh pasta sheets

½ cup (4 oz/125 g) unsalted butter, melted and kept hot

1 cup (4 oz/125 g) freshly grated Parmesan cheese, preferably Parmigiano-Reggiano

About ½ cup (2½ oz/75 g) frozen petite peas, boiled just until tender (optional)

Fresh chervil for garnish

To make the filling, in a small frying pan over medium-high heat, warm the olive oil. Add the onion and peas, reduce the heat to low, and cook, stirring, until the onion is translucent and the peas are tender and still bright green, about 5 minutes. Transfer to a blender or food processor, add the ricotta, goat cheese, egg, chives, mint, and salt and process just until blended. Transfer to a bowl, cover, and refrigerate until needed.

On a lightly floured work surface, unfold the pasta sheet(s). Using a 3-inch (7.5-cm) biscuit cutter, cut out 36 circles from the pasta.

Place a generous teaspoon of the filling on one half of each circle. Brush the edges of the circle with water. Fold the circle in half and use your fingers to press the edges together, sealing them securely.

Dust a baking sheet with flour, and place the finished agnolini on it. (The agnolini can be made up to 2 hours in advance. Leave on the baking sheet, lightly dust the tops with flour, and cover with a kitchen towel.)

Bring a large pot of salted water to a boil over high heat. In batches, gently slide in the agnolini, being careful not to crowd them. Reduce the heat to medium and cook until tender to the bite, about 6 minutes. Using a slotted spoon, transfer the agnolini to a warmed platter. Repeat until all the agnolini are cooked. Transfer to a warmed shallow bowl or individual plates, and pour the butter evenly over the top. Sprinkle with the cheese and with the peas, mint, if desired, and chervil. Serve at once.

parmesan and butternut squash ravioli with fried sage

SERVES 4–6

Parmesan, squash, and sage form a magical combination in this classic Italian pasta. Although it is time consuming to make, the result is well worth your effort. It's imperative that the squash be dry without a trace of liquid; otherwise, the stuffing will seep out the edges of the ravioli.

FOR THE FILLING

1 butternut squash,
2–2½ lb (1–1.25 kg)

1 tsp extra-virgin olive oil

1 large egg, lightly beaten

½ cup (2 oz/60 g)
freshly grated Parmesan
cheese, preferably
Parmigiano-Reggiano

1 tsp sea salt

½ tsp ground cinnamon

½ tsp ground cloves

½ tsp freshly ground pepper

All-purpose flour for dusting

12 oz (375 g) purchased
fresh pasta sheets

2 Tbsp extra-virgin olive oil

24 fresh sage leaves

1 Tbsp fresh lemon juice

½ cup (4 oz/125 g)
unsalted butter, melted

To make the filling, preheat the oven to 375°F (190°C). Cut the squash in half lengthwise and scoop out and discard the seeds and fibers. Rub the cut sides with olive oil. Place the halves, cut side down, on a rimmed baking sheet and bake until the flesh is tender when pierced with a knife, 1–1½ hours. Let cool, scoop the flesh into a bowl, and mash with a fork. If the flesh is runny, put it in a saucepan over medium-high heat and cook until dry, 3–5 minutes, then cool. Stir in the egg, cheese, salt, cinnamon, cloves, and pepper, mixing well. Cover and refrigerate until needed.

On a lightly floured work surface, unfold the pasta sheet(s). Fold in half lengthwise to mark the center, then unfold it so that it lies flat again. Place teaspoonfuls of the filling 1½ inch (4 cm) apart in a straight row down the center of one side of the fold. Dip a pastry brush in cool water and lightly brush around the filling. Fold the dough over the filling. Using your fingers, mold the dough around the filling to eliminate air pockets. Press the edges of dough together firmly to seal. Using a fluted pastry wheel, cut around the filled pasta strip, crimping the edges and trimming away about ⅛ inch (3 mm). Then, cut evenly between the mounds, making ravioli. Place the ravioli in a single layer on a lightly floured baking sheet.

Bring a large pot of salted water to a boil over high heat. In batches, gently slide in the ravioli, being careful not to crowd them. Reduce the heat to medium and cook until tender, 6–8 minutes. Using a slotted spoon, transfer the ravioli to a warmed platter and keep warm.

Meanwhile, in a frying pan over medium-high heat, warm the olive oil. Add the sage and cook until crisp, about 1 minute. Drain on paper towels. Stir the lemon juice into the melted butter and pour over the ravioli. Garnish with fried sage leaves and serve at once.

spinach lasagne with three cheeses

I like white lasagnes like this one, where the sauce is a delicate béchamel and the cheeses are the stars. The combination of the soft, almost sweet ricotta, the firm and mild mozzarella, and the strong, almost meaty *pecorino romano* gives the dish interesting texture and rich flavor.

Sea salt

2 lb (1 kg) fresh spinach, tough stems removed

1 lb (500 g) fresh whole-milk ricotta cheese

¼ cup (1½ oz/45 g) minced shallots

2 Tbsp fresh thyme leaves

1 large egg

4 Tbsp (2 oz/60 g) unsalted butter

¼ cup (1½ oz/45 g) all-purpose flour

¼ tsp freshly grated nutmeg

⅛ tsp cayenne pepper

3 cups (24 fl oz/750 ml) milk, heated

1 box (7 oz/220 g) no-boil lasagne noodles (16 noodles)

6 oz (185 g) *pecorino romano* cheese, grated

10 oz (315 g) fresh mozzarella cheese, thinly sliced

Bring a large pot of water to a boil over medium-high heat. Add 1 teaspoon salt and the spinach. Cook until the spinach is limp and tender but still bright green, 4–6 minutes. Drain and rinse under running cold water to stop the cooking. Squeeze dry to remove as much moisture as possible and chop coarsely. Squeeze dry again and set aside.

In a bowl, mix together the ricotta, shallots, thyme, egg, and ½ teaspoon salt. Set aside. In a saucepan over medium heat, melt the butter. When it foams, whisk in the flour, ½ teaspoon salt, the nutmeg, and the cayenne until a paste forms. Slowly whisk in the hot milk, reduce the heat to medium-low, and cook, whisking often, until the sauce is thickened, about 15 minutes. Remove from the heat.

Preheat the oven to 375°F (190°C). Pour a thin layer of the sauce in the bottom of a 9-by-13-inch (23-by-33-cm) baking dish. Add a single layer of 4 lasagne noodles. Top with one-third of the spinach, a thin layer of the sauce, one-third of the ricotta mixture, one-third of the romano, and one-fourth of the mozzarella. Repeat the layers twice, then top with the remaining 4 noodles. Pour over the remaining sauce, slipping a knife along the edges to ensure the sauce runs down into the pan. Top with the remaining slices of mozzarella. Bake until the sauce is bubbling, the top is brown, and the pasta is tender to the bite, about 45 minutes. Let stand for 10 minutes before serving. Cut into squares and serve at once.

orzo with feta, basil, and shrimp

In Mediterranean cuisine, feta cheese is often paired with shrimp, the creamy, salty flavors marrying lusciously. Here, I add the crumbled feta at the end of the cooking so it soaks up the warm juices from the sautéed shrimp. This dish makes a satisfying light meal or summer salad.

1 lb (500 g)
medium shrimp,
peeled and deveined

¼ cup (2 fl oz/60 ml) plus
2 Tbsp extra-virgin olive oil

½ tsp sweet Spanish paprika

¼ tsp red pepper flakes

Sea salt

3 cups (21 oz/655 g) orzo

½ cup (½ oz/15 g)
packed fresh basil leaves,
snipped into small pieces,
plus 4–6 whole leaves

¼ lb (125 g)
feta cheese, crumbled

In a bowl, combine the shrimp, ¼ cup olive oil, paprika, red pepper flakes, and ½ teaspoon salt and mix well. Cover and set aside, 1–2 hours.

Bring a large pot of salted water to a boil over high heat. Add the orzo, stir well, and cook until al dente, according to package directions.

Meanwhile, in a large frying pan over medium-high heat, warm the 2 tablespoons olive oil. Drain the shrimp, discarding the marinade, and add to the pan. Cook, turning once or twice, until the shrimp are opaque throughout, 1–2 minutes. Transfer the shrimp and any pan juices to a plate and cover to keep warm.

When the orzo is ready, drain and transfer to a warmed serving bowl. Add the shrimp and their juices and turn several times. Add the snipped basil and cheese and turn again, gently, once or twice. Garnish with the whole basil leaves and serve at once.

try different cheeses
Ricotta salata or a soft goat cheese

serve with wine
A bright, citrusy white such as Vermentino,
Albariño, or Sauvignon Blanc

fontina, chard, and green olive frittata

Fontina, a cow's milk cheese from northeastern Italy, has a delicate earthy flavor and semifirm texture. It also melts beautifully, making it a great choice for egg dishes and grilled cheese sandwiches. In this vegetarian frittata, the cheese blends well with the salty olives and tender greens.

1 bunch Swiss chard, about 1½ lb (750 g), tough stems removed

6 large eggs

2 Tbsp half-and-half

⅓ cup (1½ oz/45 g) shredded Fontina cheese

¼ cup (1½ oz/45 g) pitted green olives, coarsely chopped

¾ tsp sea salt

½ tsp freshly ground pepper

2 Tbsp unsalted butter

1 Tbsp extra-virgin olive oil

2 Tbsp finely chopped yellow onion

1 clove garlic, minced

¼ cup (⅓ oz/10 g) chopped fresh flat leaf parsley

1 tsp chopped fresh thyme

Bring a large pot of water to a boil over high heat. Add the whole chard leaves and reduce the heat to medium. Cook until the greens are tender and the ribs are easily pierced with a fork, 12–15 minutes. Rinse under running cold water, squeeze dry, and chop finely. Squeeze dry again.

In a large bowl, beat together the eggs, half-and-half, cheese, olives, salt, and pepper just until blended. Stir in the chard. In a large nonstick frying pan over medium-high heat, melt the butter with the olive oil. Add the onion and cook until translucent, 2–3 minutes. Add the garlic and cook for about 1 minute longer. Pour in the egg mixture and reduce the heat to low. As the eggs begin to set, using a spatula, lift up the edges to allow the uncooked eggs to flow underneath. Cook until the frittata is just firm around the edges and nearly set on top, 4–5 minutes. Invert a flat plate over the pan and, holding the pan and plate together, flip them. Lift off the pan, return it to the heat, and sprinkle half *each* of the parsley and thyme over the bottom. Slide the frittata, browned side up, into the pan and cook until lightly browned on the underside, 1–2 minutes longer. Remove from the heat and again invert the frittata onto the plate. Sprinkle with the remaining herbs, cut into wedges, and serve hot or warm.

serve with wine
A rich white such as Sémillon or Chenin Blanc, or a light-bodied red like Dolcetto d'Alba or Grenache

summer vegetable stacks

Along with garden-fresh tomatoes, grilled summer vegetables make an exceptional partner for buffalo mozzarella and basil. Eggplant and peppers are used here, but zucchini or summer squash would work as well. This colorful stack also makes an elegant starter.

4 small eggplants,
sliced lengthwise into
3 pieces each

2 red bell peppers,
seeded and cut lengthwise
into quarters

¼ cup (2 fl oz/60 ml)
extra-virgin olive oil,
plus more for drizzling

2 Tbsp balsamic vinegar

1 tsp sea salt, plus more
for sprinkling

½ tsp freshly ground pepper,
plus more for sprinkling

8 large heirloom
tomato slices

2–3 balls fresh mozzarella
cheese, preferably buffalo's
milk, cut into 8 slices

Handful of torn fresh
basil leaves

Place the eggplant slices and bell pepper quarters in a bowl and add the olive oil, vinegar, salt, and pepper. Turn several times, then let stand for 30–60 minutes, turning once or twice. Meanwhile, preheat a grill to medium-high and oil the grill rack.

Arrange the eggplant slices and bell peppers directly on the grill rack or in a single layer in a grilling basket. Cook until the eggplants and the peppers are lightly charred, 6–7 minutes for the eggplants and about 4 minutes for the peppers. Turn and cook until the second sides are browned and charred. The timing will be about the same. Transfer the eggplant slices to a platter. Put the peppers in a resealable plastic bag, seal closed, and let cool. When cool enough to handle, peel away the charred skin with your fingertips.

To assemble each stack, place a tomato slice on each plate, then stack the remaining ingredients on top in the following order: cheese, eggplant, bell pepper, tomato, cheese, eggplant, bell pepper, and eggplant, seasoning the layers with salt and pepper. Drizzle with olive oil and garnish with the basil leaves. Serve at once.

try different cheeses
Feta, *burrata,* or grilled *halloumi* will work nicely here

serve with wine
A high-acid, crisp white like Muscadet, Soave, or Pinot Bianco,
or Tempranillo for red

cheese enchiladas

I first learned to make enchiladas from scratch when I was eleven, and I always make my own sauce using ancho chiles. As far as I'm concerned, the cheesier the better. Cotija, a crumbly, hard Mexican cheese, mixed with Jack or Cheddar yields the best results.

2 cups (16 fl oz/500 ml)
low-sodium beef broth,
heated to boiling

5 ancho chiles

Corn or canola oil for frying

¾ cup (3 oz/90 g)
chopped white onion

4 cloves garlic, minced

1 can (28 oz/875 g)
whole tomatoes, with juice

2 tsp chopped
fresh oregano

½ tsp *each* ground cumin
and chipotle chile powder

Sea salt

12 corn tortillas, 8 inches
(20 cm) in diameter

3 cups (12 oz/375 g)
shredded Monterey Jack
or mild Cheddar cheese

6 green onions, minced

¾ lb (375 g)
Cotija cheese, crumbled

⅓ cup (2 oz/60 g)
sliced olives (optional)

In a heatproof bowl, combine the hot broth and chiles and let stand until the chiles are soft, 8–10 minutes. Drain, reserving the broth. Seed the chiles and coarsely chop.

In a frying pan over medium-high heat, warm 2 tablespoons oil. Add the onion and cook until translucent, 2–3 minutes. Add the garlic and cook for 1 minute. Transfer the mixture to a blender, add the tomatoes and their juice, the chopped chiles, the oregano, and the cumin and process until smooth. Return the mixture to the frying pan over medium heat and cook, stirring, until it thickens and bubbles, about 2 minutes. Stir in the chipotle chile and 1 cup (8 fl oz/250 ml) of the reserved broth and season with salt. Cook for 1–2 minutes, then taste and adjust the seasoning. Continue to cook, stirring occasionally, until thickened but still pourable, about 10 minutes. Remove from the heat and pour a thin layer of the sauce in the bottom of an 8-by-12-inch (20-by-30-cm) baking dish.

Preheat the oven to 375°F (190°C). Pour a thin film of oil into a frying pan placed over medium heat. Add a tortilla and heat for a few seconds until softened. Using tongs, transfer the tortilla to the baking dish. Sprinkle about 2 tablespoons of the Jack and some green onions down the center, roll up, and place, seam side down, at one end of the dish. Repeat to fill all the remaining tortillas, then pour the remaining sauce over them, covering completely, and top with the remaining Jack. Bake until the cheese melts and the tortillas have absorbed the sauce, about 25 minutes. Remove from the oven, top with the Cotija and the olives, if desired. Serve at once.

grilled serrano ham and manchego sandwich

I've never met a ham and cheese sandwich I didn't like, and this Spanish-inspired version is exceptional. It features the classic pairing of Manchego and *membrillo* (quince paste). Manchego is available at various stages of aging; I prefer a semiaged cheese here, but any will do.

8 slices ciabatta, sturdy white bread, or whole-grain bread

4 Tbsp (2 oz/60 g) unsalted butter, at room temperature

5–6 oz (155–185 g) semiaged Manchego cheese, thinly sliced

¼ lb (125 g) thinly sliced serrano ham (8 slices)

¼ lb (125 g) *membrillo* (see note), cut into 4 thin slices

Spread 1 side of each bread slice with a little of the butter. Place 4 slices, buttered side up, on a work surface. Top the bread with the Manchego, covering it completely. Place 2 slices of ham on each sandwich, and then 1 slice of *membrillo*. Top the sandwiches with the remaining bread slices, buttered side up.

In a large frying pan or griddle over medium-high heat, add the sandwiches, buttered side down, and then spread the tops with the remaining butter. Cook until the undersides are golden brown, 4–5 minutes. Using a spatula, turn the sandwiches, then press down for 20–30 seconds. Cook until golden brown on the second side, about 4 minutes longer.

Transfer to individual plates or a platter. Cut into halves or quarters and serve at once.

try different cheeses
Idiazábal, Fontina, or Montasio

serve with wine
Rioja or Tempranillo for red, Verdejo or Albariño for white

herbed pork involtini with pecorino

Involtini, thin slices of meat filled, rolled, and tied before cooking, are an Italian favorite. Fillings can vary from a simple bread-and-herb mix to more exotic flavors. When I make this dish, I like to add pancetta or prosciutto to the filling—along with plenty of cheese.

8 slices pork loin, each about ¼ inch (6 mm) thick

¾ cup (1½ oz/45 g) fresh bread crumbs

¾ cup (3 oz/90 g) grated pecorino cheese

¼ cup (⅓ oz/10 g) minced fresh flat-leaf parsley

2 Tbsp minced fresh sage, plus 8 whole leaves

1 Tbsp minced fresh thyme

Sea salt and freshly ground pepper

1 large egg plus 1 egg yolk

8 slices pancetta or bacon

½ cup (4 oz/125 g) unsalted butter

All-purpose flour for dusting

1½ cups (12 fl oz/375 ml) dry white wine such as Sauvignon Blanc

One at a time, place the pork slices between 2 sheets of waxed paper. Using a meat pounder, pound until a uniform ⅛ inch (3 mm) thick. In a bowl, combine the bread crumbs, cheese, parsley, minced sage, thyme, ¾ teaspoon salt, and ½ teaspoon pepper. Add the egg and egg yolk and mix together to make a sticky mass. Lay a slice of pancetta down the center of each pork slice. Top with about one-eighth of the filling, spreading it beyond the pancetta slightly. Fold in both sides of the pork slice to cover the stuffing partially, then roll up the pork, holding the edges as you work to keep the roll snug. Place a sage leaf lengthwise on the roll, then secure the roll and the leaf with 3 bands of kitchen string. Repeat with the remaining pork slices.

In a Dutch oven or other heavy-bottomed pan just large enough to hold the rolls in a single layer, melt the butter over medium-high heat. Place a colander over a plate or bowl. Put 2 pork rolls in the colander and sprinkle with a few tablespoons of flour. Shake the colander, leaving only a light dusting of flour on the rolls. Transfer to a plate and repeat to flour the other pork rolls. Add the rolls to the pan and cook, turning as needed, until browned on all sides and firm when pressed with your fingertip, about 10 minutes. Transfer the rolls to a plate. Add the wine, scraping up any bits clinging to the bottom of the pan. Stir in ¼ teaspoon salt and ½ teaspoon pepper and return the rolls to the pan. Reduce the heat to low, cover, and cook, turning the rolls twice, until the liquid reduces to a thick sauce, about 15 minutes. Transfer the rolls to a platter. Snip the strings and serve hot. Pass the sauce at the table.

lamb kebabs with warm feta, grilled tomato, and eggplant

SERVES 6–8

Feta, which can be made from the milk of goats, sheep, or cows, or a combination thereof, is almost always found on the daily table of the eastern Mediterranean, along with lamb, tomatoes, and eggplant. Here, I've combined these menu staples into a single main course.

FOR THE LAMB

¼ cup (2 fl oz/60 ml) extra-virgin olive oil

3 cloves garlic, crushed

1 tsp dried oregano or 1 Tbsp chopped fresh oregano

½ tsp sea salt

½ tsp freshly ground black pepper

½ tsp red pepper flakes

2 lb (1 kg) boneless lamb shoulder or leg, cut into 1½-inch (4-cm) cubes

FOR THE SIDES

¼ cup (2 fl oz/60 ml) extra-virgin olive oil

1 clove garlic, minced

½ tsp each sea salt and freshly ground pepper

8 tomatoes, halved

4 small eggplants, halved lengthwise, or 1 large eggplant, sliced lengthwise ½ inch (12 mm) thick

½ lb (250 g) firm feta cheese, cut into ½-inch (12-mm) cubes

To marinate the lamb, in a bowl, whisk together the olive oil, garlic, oregano, salt, black pepper, and red pepper flakes. Add the lamb and turn to coat. Cover and refrigerate for at least 1 hour or up to 4 hours.

Prepare the vegetables and the cheese 2–3 hours before cooking. In a bowl, combine the olive oil, garlic, salt, and pepper. Place the tomatoes, cut side up, in a shallow baking dish and brush with the olive oil mixture. Do the same with the eggplant, but brush on both sides. Place the cheese in the bowl with the remaining olive oil mixture and turn gently to coat.

Preheat a grill to medium-high and oil the grill rack. Have ready 16–18 skewers; if using wooden skewers, first soak in water for 10 minutes. Remove the lamb from the marinade and thread 3–4 pieces on each skewer. Place the eggplants on the grill rack and grill, turning once, until golden brown on both sides, 5–6 minutes on each side. Transfer to a platter and cover to keep warm. Place the lamb skewers on the grill rack and grill, turning as needed, until nicely browned on all sides and tender, about 15 minutes. About 10 minutes before the lamb is done, place the tomatoes in a grilling basket and grill, turning as needed, until lightly charred, about 10 minutes.

Arrange the lamb skewers, tomatoes, eggplants, and cheese on 1 or more platters and serve at once.

roast chicken stuffed with gruyère, bread, and sausage

SERVES 4–6

Gruyère is a good cheese to use for stuffing and for gratins because it both melts evenly and retains its essential character, adding that essence to the dish at hand. Here, it contributes extra flavor and texture to a traditional bread-and-sausage stuffing for roast chicken.

FOR THE STUFFING

2 Tbsp unsalted butter

2 Tbsp minced shallots

2 tsp minced fresh thyme

½ tsp sea salt

½ tsp freshly ground pepper

¼ lb (125 g) bulk pork or chicken sausage

3 oz (90 g) Gruyère cheese, cut into ¼-inch (6-mm) cubes

3–4 baguette slices, each 1 inch (2.5 cm) thick, cut into 1-inch (2.5-cm) cubes

2 tsp chopped fresh flat-leaf parsley

About 1½ cups (12 fl oz/375 ml) low-sodium chicken broth

1 chicken, about 4 lb (2 kg)

1 Tbsp unsalted butter, at room temperature

½ tsp sea salt

½ tsp freshly ground pepper

Preheat the oven to 350°F (180°C). Choose a roasting pan just large enough to accommodate the chicken, and place a rack in the pan.

To make the stuffing, in a frying pan over medium heat, melt the butter. When the butter foams, add the shallots, thyme, salt, and pepper and cook, stirring, until the shallots are translucent, about 2 minutes. Add the sausage and cook, stirring occasionally, until just softened, about 5 minutes. Transfer the mixture to a bowl and add the cheese, bread cubes, and parsley. Moisten with the chicken broth, adding just enough to bind the mixture together in a slightly sticky mass.

Pat the chicken dry and rub inside and out with the butter. Season with the salt and pepper. Pack the cavity snugly with the stuffing and truss the legs with kitchen string. Place the stuffed bird on the rack and roast until the skin is golden brown and the juices of the inner thigh run clear when pierced with a knife, or until an instant-read thermometer inserted into the thigh without touching bone registers 160°F (71°C), about 1½ hours. Transfer to a cutting board, cover loosely with aluminum foil, and let rest for 10–15 minutes before carving.

To serve, scoop the stuffing from the cavity onto a platter. Carve the chicken into serving pieces and arrange them around the stuffing. Drizzle with juices from the roasting pan and serve at once.

cheese lover's burger

Like everyone I know, I succumb to a big, juicy cheeseburger. For a fun twist, I'll tuck cheese into the center of the meat patties where it melts as the meat cooks. My favorite cheese to use is Cheddar or Gorgonzola. Topping the burger with extra cheese makes it simply irresistible.

3 lb (1.5 kg) ground chuck

1 Tbsp sea salt

1½ tsp freshly ground pepper

3 oz (90 g) Gorgonzola *dolce* cheese, plus more for topping

6 hamburger buns, split

SUGGESTED EXTRAS

Butter lettuce leaves or arugula

Tomato slices

Purple onion slices, grilled or raw

Roasted red bell pepper slices

Pepperoncini

In a bowl, combine the meat, salt, and pepper and mix together with your hands. Divide the meat into 12 balls and flatten 6 of them slightly. Divide the Gorgonzola into 6 portions. In the center of each of the 6 slightly flattened balls, place a cheese portion. Place the remaining balls of meat on top and pinch the edges together. Gently flatten to make 6 patties 5–6 inches (13–15 cm) in diameter. Wrap in plastic wrap and refrigerate for at least 1 hour or up to 4 hours before cooking.

Preheat a grill to medium-high and oil the grill rack. Place the buns, cut side down, on the grill and grill until just golden, 2–3 minutes. Transfer to a plate and keep warm. Place the patties on the grill and cook for about 4 minutes per side for rare, 6–8 minutes per side for medium, and a full 10 minutes per side for well done. During the last minute of cooking, add more Gorgonzola to the top of each burger.

Serve the burgers hot with the buns and condiments.

═══════════════ ◉ ═══════════════

try different cheeses
Pepper Jack, Swiss, Fontina, Boucheron, Camembert, or Gruyère

serve with wine or beer
A medium-bodied red such as Syrah or pale ale

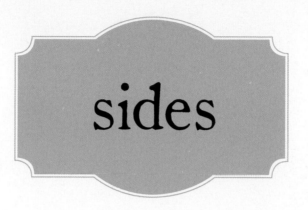

sides

At my table, sides are as important as main
courses, so I give them equal attention, which
often means adding cheese. Slices of fresh mozzarella
or slabs of Saint Marcellin contribute a welcome
complexity to roasted or grilled vegetables, and
broccoli, asparagus, or potatoes, fresh from my garden,
are always special when baked with a cheese sauce.
And no one, especially me, can resist a lofty cheese
soufflé or a batch of cheese-laced corn fritters.

oven-roasted endive
with saint-marcellin

Named after the town of Saint-Marcellin near Grenoble in the French Alps, this cow's milk cheese is usually eaten fresh. It's sold in a round terra-cotta dish that you might like to keep for another use. Tangy and creamy, it's scrumptious melted over endive—if not eaten from a spoon.

2½ Tbsp unsalted butter, cut into small pieces, plus more for greasing

5 large or 10 small heads Belgian endive

4 slices thick-cut bacon, cut crosswise into pieces ½ inch (12 mm) wide

2 yellow onions, thinly sliced

½ tsp sea salt

½ tsp freshly ground pepper

2 Saint-Marcellin cheeses, cut into slices ½ inch (12 mm) thick

1 tsp fresh thyme leaves

Preheat the oven to 350°F (180°C). Butter a shallow baking dish. Cut each endive in half lengthwise and then cut away most of the solid base from each half, leaving only enough to hold the half together. Arrange them, cut side up, in a single, tightly packed layer in the baking dish. Dot with the 2½ tablespoons butter. Set aside.

In a sauté pan over medium heat, fry the bacon just until it begins to render its fat, then add the onions and cook until the onions are translucent and the bacon starts to crisp, about 10 minutes. Season with the salt and pepper. Spoon the bacon-onion mixture on top of the endives, tucking it in around them. Top with the cheese and sprinkle with the thyme leaves.

Bake until the cheese is fully melted and lightly golden, about 20 minutes. Serve hot.

try different cheeses
Gruyère, Swiss, Emmentaler, Cheddar, Taleggio, or Fontina (grate, rather than slice, firmer cheeses)

polenta with white cheddar, chard, and wild mushrooms

SERVES 4–6

This dish is a standby in my kitchen, especially when my garden is full of chard. It makes an excellent vegetarian dish, and the cheese infuses the polenta with such flavor that it could be eaten on its own, even without the vegetable topping. Parmesan or Fontina work well, too.

Sea salt and freshly
ground pepper

1½ cups (10½ oz/330 g)
polenta

2 bunches chard,
tough stems removed

1 lb (500 g) assorted
wild mushrooms such as
chanterelles, porcini, morels,
or lobster mushrooms,
cleaned and coarsely cut
or left whole depending
on size

1 fresh rosemary sprig,
about 6 inches (15 cm) long

1 Tbsp extra-virgin olive oil

4 Tbsp (2 oz/60 g)
unsalted butter

1 Tbsp minced shallots

1 cup (4 oz/125 g)
white Cheddar cheese,
shredded or crumbled

In a large saucepan over high heat, bring 8 cups (64 fl oz/2 l) water and 1½ teaspoons salt to a boil. Add the polenta in a slow, steady stream, stirring constantly. Reduce the heat to low and cook, stirring often, until the polenta pulls away from the sides of the pan, 40–45 minutes.

Meanwhile, prepare the chard and mushrooms. Bring a large pot of water to a boil over high heat. Add the chard leaves, folding them to fit, and the rosemary sprig. Reduce the heat to medium and cook until the chard ribs are easily pierced with a fork, about 15 minutes. Drain well. Chop coarsely and squeeze dry. Set aside.

In a frying pan over medium-high heat, warm the olive oil and 1 tablespoon of the butter. Add the shallots and mushrooms and cook until the mushrooms are tender, 8–10 minutes. Using a slotted spoon, transfer to a bowl. Reserve the juices.

When the polenta is ready, stir in the remaining 3 tablespoons butter, all but ¼ cup (1 oz/30 g) of the cheese, 1 teaspoon salt, and 1 teaspoon pepper and cook until the butter and cheese have melted, 3–4 minutes longer. Return the frying pan you cooked the mushrooms in to medium-high heat. Warm the juices, then add the chard and mushrooms and cook, stirring, until hot and well coated with the juices. Season with ½ teaspoons each of salt and pepper.

Spoon the polenta into a large serving bowl, top with the chard and mushrooms, and sprinkle with the remaining cheese. Serve at once.

roasted winter squash purée with blue cheese

As soon as it is in season, I start to cook with winter squash, which can be paired with countless different seasonings and ingredients, from sweet to savory. I've found that adding a mild blue cheese, such as Fourme d'Ambert, brings out the earthy-sweetness of the squash.

2 lb (1 kg) winter squash, such as butternut or acorn, or Sugar Pie pumpkin

2 Tbsp extra-virgin olive oil

1 Tbsp heavy cream, plus more if needed

1 Tbsp unsalted butter, at room temperature

¼ tsp sea salt

½ tsp freshly ground pepper, plus more for sprinkling

3 oz (90 g) mild, soft blue cheese, plus crumbled cheese for garnish, at room temperature

Preheat the oven to 350°F (180°C). Halve the squash, discarding the seeds and fibers. Place the squash pieces on a rimmed baking sheet and drizzle with 1 tablespoon of the olive oil. Turn the pieces over and drizzle with the remaining 1 tablespoon olive oil. Cover tightly with aluminum foil and bake until the flesh is easily pierced with a fork, about 1 hour.

Remove the squash from the oven and, when cool enough to handle, scoop the flesh into a bowl. Add the cream, butter, salt, pepper, and 3 ounces blue cheese and, using an electric mixer, purée until fluffy. Add more cream if necessary for a smooth consistency. Taste and adjust the seasoning if needed.

Just before serving, return the purée to a saucepan over medium heat and heat, stirring, until hot, 3–4 minutes. Spoon into a serving bowl, garnish with the crumbled blue cheese, and sprinkle with pepper. Serve hot.

try different cheeses
Coarsely grated Parmesan or Fontina, or cubed Taleggio

broccoli with cheese sauce

Broccoli with cheese sauce is a longtime American favorite, served at countless tables throughout the country. You can vary the flavor by using different cheeses, such as Swiss or Fontina, but a good, sharp Cheddar is my hands-down favorite choice for this comfort-food dish.

4–5 large heads broccoli

3 Tbsp unsalted butter

3 Tbsp all-purpose flour

2 cups (16 fl oz/500 ml) whole milk

½ tsp sea salt

½ tsp freshly ground black pepper

⅛ tsp cayenne pepper

3 oz (90 g) sharp Cheddar cheese, grated

Trim the thick stalks from the broccoli heads and discard. Cut the heads lengthwise into halves or thirds, depending on size. Bring water to a boil in a steamer pan. Arrange the broccoli on the steamer rack, place over the boiling water, cover, and steam until easily pierced with a fork, about 15 minutes. Drain, and cover to keep warm.

Meanwhile, make the sauce. In a saucepan over medium-high heat, melt the butter. When it foams, remove the pan from the heat and whisk in the flour to make a thick paste. Return to the heat and slowly pour in the milk, whisking constantly. Bring to a boil, continuing to whisk. Reduce the heat to low and simmer, stirring occasionally, until slightly thickened, 7–10 minutes. Stir in the salt, black pepper, and cayenne and continue to simmer, stirring occasionally, until the mixture has thickened, enough to coat the back of a spoon, about 10 minutes longer. Add the cheese and stir just until melted, about 2 minutes. Remove from the heat.

Arrange the broccoli pieces in a warmed serving bowl and pour the hot sauce over them. Serve at once.

⊙

try different cheeses
Any semifirm, sharp cheese such as Gruyère or Monterey Jack

cheese grits

I had never eaten grits until a good friend from Kentucky sent me a
package of stone-ground grits and a recipe. I fell in love with them and
now serve them regularly, often in place of potatoes, rice, or polenta.
I like using two different Cheddars for a more complex flavor.

½ Tbsp unsalted butter

3 large eggs

1 cup (8 fl oz/250 ml)
whole milk

1 tsp sea salt

¾ cup (4 oz/125 g) grits

1 cup (4 oz/125 g)
shredded white
Cheddar cheese

1 cup (4 oz/125 g)
shredded sharp
Cheddar cheese

½ cup (1½ oz/45 g)
minced green onions

Freshly ground pepper

Preheat the oven to 325°F (165°C). Butter a 2-quart (2-l) baking dish
with the butter. In a bowl, whisk together the eggs and milk until well
blended. Set the mixture aside.

In a saucepan over medium-high heat, combine 2 cups (16 fl oz/
500 ml) water and the salt and bring to a boil. Slowly stir in the grits.
Reduce the heat to low, cover the pan, and cook, stirring often, until the
grits are soft and the water is absorbed, about 20 minutes. Remove from
the heat, cover, and let stand for 5 minutes to thicken.

Spoon the hot grits into a bowl and add the egg mixture, whisking until
blended. Whisk in about three-fourths of each cheese, the green onions,
and pepper to taste, and mix well. Pour the grits into the prepared baking
dish and sprinkle with the remaining cheese.

Bake until the edges are brown and a toothpick inserted into the middle
comes out clean, about 20 minutes. Serve at once.

try different cheeses
Monterey Jack, Parmesan, or Fontina

grill-roasted tomatoes topped with cheese and herbs

SERVES 4

From the time the first fruit ripens to that last, sad moment when the frost arrives, tomatoes are an essential part of my summer garden and daily table. Since I grill often, this dish—which is like a warm, oozy *insalata caprese*—has become a regular side dish.

6 oz (185 g)
fresh mozzarella
cheese, sliced

2 Tbsp extra-virgin olive oil,
plus more for drizzling

Salt and freshly
ground pepper

4 tomatoes,
cut in half crosswise

½ cup (½ oz/15 g)
fresh basil leaves

In a bowl, toss the mozzarella slices with 2 tablespoons olive oil. Sprinkle with salt and pepper.

Preheat a grill to medium-high and oil the grill rack. Place the tomatoes, cut side up, in a grilling basket, or place on the grill cut side up, cover the grill, and cook until the skin begins to wrinkle, about 10 minutes. Add a basil leaf or two and a slice of mozzarella to the top of each tomato half and continue to grill, covered, until the cheese starts to soften, about 2 minutes longer.

Transfer to a serving platter, drizzle with olive oil, and season with salt and pepper. Serve at once.

try different cheeses
Thinly sliced blue, *halloumi,* or feta or grated Cheddar or Jack

smashed fingerlings
with fromage blanc

Fromage blanc is a creamy, slightly tangy fresh cheese that originated in Belgium. It is delicious swirled into soups, drizzled with honey, or mixed with vegetables, like these tender fingerling potatoes, which are smashed just a bit and then mixed with the cheese and spring chives.

2 lb (1 kg)
fingerling potatoes

1 tsp sea salt

2 Tbsp unsalted butter

¼ cup (2 oz/60 g)
fromage blanc

½ tsp freshly ground pepper

1 Tbsp minced fresh chives

In a large saucepan over high heat, combine the potatoes and salt and add water to cover by 2 inches (5 cm). Bring to a boil. Reduce the heat to medium, cover, and cook until the potatoes are tender when pierced with a sharp knife, 20–25 minutes.

Drain the potatoes and return them to the pan. Add the butter. Using a fork or the back of a wooden spoon, crush the potatoes, breaking them into large, fluffy chunks. Add the cheese and pepper to the potatoes and crush a few more times to blend in the cheese. Taste and adjust the seasoning with salt and pepper. Transfer the potatoes to a warmed serving bowl and garnish with the chives. Serve at once.

try different cheeses
Fresh ricotta or soft goat cheese

grilled radicchio with scamorza

Scamorza is primarily made in northern Italy, commonly from cow's milk, and is available smoked. Its mild, milky taste is similar to mozzarella or provolone. I serve this side with roasted pork, which stands up well to the wonderfully smoky flavor of the grilled radicchio.

2 small to medium
heads radicchio

2 Tbsp extra-virgin olive oil

1 tsp fresh lemon juice

1½ tsp sea salt

½ tsp freshly ground pepper

Canola oil for grilling

6 oz (185 g) *scamorza*
cheese, shredded

Remove any damaged outer leaves from the radicchio. Cut each head lengthwise through the core into slices about 1½ inches (4 cm) thick, making sure that each slice has a bit of the core attached to hold it together during cooking. (The end slices, which will not be attached to the core, can be reserved for another use, such as salad.) Put the radicchio slices in a single layer in a shallow dish. Drizzle with 1 tablespoon of the olive oil and ½ teaspoon of the lemon juice. Season with half each of the salt and pepper. Turn the slices over and repeat the drizzling and seasoning on the other side. Let stand at room temperature for at least 30 minutes or up to 4 hours before grilling.

When ready to cook, preheat the oven to 325°F (165°C). Oil a grill pan and warm over medium-high heat. Place the radicchio slices in the grill pan and cook until seared and golden on the first side, 3–4 minutes. Turn the radicchio over and grill for 1–2 minutes longer. Transfer the radicchio to a baking dish and top with the cheese, dividing it evenly. Bake until the cheese has melted, about 4 minutes. Serve hot.

try different cheeses
Muenster, *crescenza*, Port-Salut, Taleggio, or any mild melting cheese

bread pudding with asparagus and fontina cheese

Slivers of Fontina cheese are dotted throughout this savory pudding and offer bursts of rich flavor; the Romano brings a hit of chewy saltiness. Save up your leftover bread for a week, including baguette heels; heavy breads make a dense pudding; lighter ones yield a softer texture.

8–12 thick slices stale bread, each slice cut in half

2½ cups (20 fl oz/625 ml) whole milk, plus more if needed

5 large eggs

1 tsp sea salt

1 tsp freshly ground pepper

1 lb (500 g) asparagus, tough ends removed, and cut on the diagonal into 2-inch (5-cm) lengths

½ cup (¾ oz/20 g) chopped mixed fresh herbs such as chives, flat-leaf parsley, tarragon, thyme, and marjoram

¼ cup (1 oz/30 g) freshly grated Romano cheese

½ lb (250 g) Fontina cheese, slivered

½ Tbsp unsalted butter, cut into small pieces

Place the bread in a shallow dish and pour the milk over the top. Let soak until the bread has absorbed the milk and softened. Depending on the hardness of the bread, this will take from 5–30 minutes. Squeeze the bread slices to extract the milk. Measure the milk extracted; you should have ½ cup (4 fl oz/125 ml). If not, make up the difference with additional milk. Set the bread and milk aside separately.

Preheat the oven to 350°F (180°C). Butter one large 12-inch (30-cm) shallow baking dish or two smaller 8-inch (20-cm) shallow baking dishes or ramekins. In a bowl, beat together the eggs, salt, pepper, and reserved milk until well blended. Arrange the bread in the prepared baking dish. Set 6–8 asparagus tips aside and top the bread with the remaining asparagus and the mixed herbs. Sprinkle the cheeses over the asparagus. Pour the milk-egg mixture over the top, and dot with the butter. Bake until the top is crusty brown and a knife inserted into the middle of the pudding comes out clean, about 45 minutes. During the last 5 minutes of cooking, top with the reserved asparagus tips. Let the pudding stand for 15 minutes before serving.

try different cheeses
Parmesan and Gruyère, or any combination of mild melting cheeses

spinach and cheese timbales

These delicate and savory custards make an unusual side dish. I serve them alongside roasted meat or, with the addition of a swirl of tomato sauce on top, as a first course. You can substitute chard or kale for the spinach, though both need to cook 5 minutes longer to become tender.

1 bunch spinach,
about 12 oz (375 g),
tough stems removed

4 large eggs

1½ cups (12 fl oz/375 ml)
whole milk, hot

⅓ cup (¾ oz/20 g)
fresh bread crumbs

½ cup (2 oz/60 g)
shredded Cheddar cheese

1 tsp minced yellow onion

½ tsp sea salt

¼ tsp freshly ground pepper

2 tsp unsalted butter

Preheat the oven to 325°F (165°C). Place the spinach in a large saucepan and add 2 inches (5 cm) of water. Place over high heat and cook until the spinach is tender but still bright green, about 5 minutes. Drain and rinse under running cold water. Squeeze dry, then mince. Squeeze dry again and set aside. You should have about ½ cup (3½ oz/105 g) minced spinach. In a large bowl, whisk the eggs, then mix in the milk, bread crumbs, cheese, spinach, onion, salt, and pepper.

Butter eight ½–¾ cup (4–6 fl oz/125–180 ml) custard cups or similar ovenproof dishes. Or, butter a 9-inch (23-cm) gratin dish. Divide the milk mixture evenly among the cups or pour into the dish. Place the cups or dish in a baking pan. Pour hot water into the pan to reach halfway up the sides of the cups or dish.

Bake until a toothpick inserted into the middle comes out clean and the surface is lightly golden, 40–50 minutes. To serve the cups, remove from the water bath and let cool, about 10 minutes. Run a thin-bladed knife around the inside edge of a cup, invert a serving plate over the cup, invert the plate and cup together, and lift off the cup. To serve the gratin dish, unmold the same way onto a platter, and cut into slices to serve at once.

try different cheeses
A semihard grating cheese such as Gruyère,
dry Jack, or Comté

manchego and jalapeño biscuits

Manchego is a dry and flavorful cheese made from the milk of Manchega sheep in the La Mancha region of Spain. I like to serve these cheesy, jalapeño-flecked biscuits with bold-flavored dishes, such as barbecued ribs, roast pork shoulder, or chili con carne.

2 cups (10 oz/315 g) all-purpose flour, plus more for dusting

1 Tbsp baking powder

1 tsp sea salt

1 jalapeño chile, seeded and minced

3 oz (90 g) aged Manchego cheese, grated

6 Tbsp (3 oz/90 g) cold unsalted butter, cut into small pieces

¾ cup (6 fl oz/180 ml) plus 2 Tbsp whole milk

Preheat the oven to 450°F (230°C). In a large bowl, whisk together the flour, baking powder, salt, chile, and cheese. Scatter the butter over the top. Using a pastry blender or 2 knives, cut the butter into the flour mixture until the butter pieces are the size of peas. Pour the milk into the flour mixture. Using a fork, turn just until the dry ingredients are moistened. With your hands, gather the dough into a rough ball and knead a few times in the bowl.

On a lightly floured work surface, roll out the dough into a round about ½ inch (12 mm) thick. Using a round biscuit cutter about 1¼ inches (3 cm) in diameter, cut out as many rounds as you can and place them on a baking sheet. Gather together the scraps, roll out again, cut out as many rounds as you can, and add to the baking sheet.

Bake until the biscuits have puffed slightly and the tops are lightly golden, about 10 minutes. Serve at once.

try different cheeses
A sharp or medium-sharp Cheddar

fresh corn and teleme fritters

Made in San Luis Obispo, California, by a family-owned company, Teleme melts well and has a slightly tart taste, making it a natural choice for binding together fresh corn and a seasoned batter. When you bite into these fritters, the oozing cheese is a delicious surprise.

4 ears corn, white, yellow, or a mixture

¼ yellow onion

¼ cup (1½ oz/45 g) all-purpose flour

½ tsp baking powder

¼ tsp sea salt, plus more for sprinkling

¼ tsp freshly ground pepper

1 large egg, lightly beaten

3 oz (90 g) Teleme cheese, cut into small cubes

Extra-virgin olive oil for frying

Hold 1 ear of corn upright, base down, in a shallow bowl. Using a sharp knife, cut straight down between the kernels and the cob, freeing the kernels and rotating the ear a quarter turn after each stroke. Repeat with the remaining ears. Transfer the corn kernels to a bowl. Using the fine rasps on a grater, grate the onion into the bowl. Sprinkle the corn and onion with the flour, baking powder, salt, and pepper and stir to mix. Add the egg and cheese and mix well.

Pour olive oil to a depth of a scant ¼ inch (6 mm) in a large frying pan and heat over medium-high heat. When the oil is hot, drop the corn mixture by heaping teaspoons into the hot oil, spacing them about 1 inch (2.5 cm) apart. Press down gently with the back of a wooden spoon and fry until golden brown on the first side, about 2 minutes. Turn the fritters and fry until golden brown on the second side, about 1 minute longer. Using a slotted spatula, transfer to a paper towel–lined platter to drain. Repeat with the remaining corn mixture, adding more oil and reducing the heat if necessary.

Transfer to a platter, sprinkle with salt, and serve hot or warm.

try different cheeses
Monterey Jack, Port-Salut, or Muenster

gruyère and parmesan soufflé

SERVES 4–6

A menu staple of French cooks, light, airy cheese soufflés melt deliciously in the mouth. To help these soufflés rise, butter the rim of the mold well, and mix one-third of the whites into the sauce, while still hot, before folding the sauce into the remaining whites.

4 Tbsp (2 oz/60 g) unsalted butter

7 large eggs

¼ cup (1½ oz/45 g) all-purpose flour

1 cup (8 fl oz/250 ml) whole milk, heated

1 tsp sea salt

½ tsp freshly ground pepper

¾ cup (3 oz/90 g) shredded Gruyère cheese

¼ cup (1 oz/30 g) freshly grated Parmesan cheese, preferably Parmigiano-Reggiano

¼ tsp cream of tartar

Preheat the oven to 350°F (180°C). Butter a 6-cup (48–fl oz/1.5-l) soufflé mold with 1 tablespoon of the butter. Refrigerate for 10 minutes. Separate the eggs, putting 4 yolks in a small bowl and all the whites in a large bowl. Bring the yolks and whites to room temperature. Save the extra yolks for another use.

In a saucepan over low heat, melt the remaining 3 tablespoons butter. When it foams, stir in the flour and cook, stirring, about 1 minute. Add the hot milk, salt, and pepper, raise the heat to medium, and bring to a boil, whisking constantly. Reduce the heat to low and boil, whisking constantly, about 1 minute. Remove from the heat, add the egg yolks, Gruyère, and Parmesan and whisk to mix well. Set aside.

Using a balloon whisk or an electric mixer, beat the egg whites with the cream of tartar until stiff peaks form. Using a spatula, gently fold one-third of the egg whites into the cheese mixture, then fold the cheese mixture gently but quickly into the remaining egg whites.

Pour the mixture into the chilled soufflé mold and place on a baking sheet. Bake until puffy and golden and a toothpick inserted into the center comes out clean, about 30 minutes. Serve at once.

try different cheeses
Gouda, Roquefort, aged goat cheese, Parmesan, or Cheddar

cauliflower gratin with two cheeses

SERVES 6–8

Gratins, with their crunchy toppings and oozy interiors, are often made with cheese. For this creamy dish, I use two French cheeses: ever-versatile Gruyère and an aged Mimolette, a lesser-known orange-hued cow's milk cheese that shreds easily and melts well.

4 Tbsp (2 oz/60 g) unsalted butter, plus more for greasing

1 head cauliflower, cut into florets

¼ cup (1½ oz/45 g) all-purpose flour

3 cups (24 fl oz/750 ml) whole milk

Pinch of cayenne pepper

½ tsp sea salt, or to taste

2 oz (60 g) Gruyère cheese, shredded

2 oz (60 g) aged Mimolette cheese, shredded

Preheat the oven to 375°F (190°C). Butter a shallow baking dish. Bring water to a boil in a steamer pan. Arrange the cauliflower florets on the steamer rack, place over the boiling water, cover, and steam until tender when pierced with a fork, about 15 minutes. Do not overcook. Remove the florets from the steamer and arrange snugly in a single layer in the prepared baking dish. Set aside.

Meanwhile, make the sauce. In a saucepan over medium-high heat, melt the 4 tablespoons butter. When it foams, remove the pan from the heat and whisk in the flour to make a thick paste. Return to the heat and slowly add the milk, whisking constantly. Add the cayenne and ½ teaspoon salt, reduce the heat to medium, and simmer, stirring occasionally, until the sauce is thick enough to coat the back of a spoon, about 15 minutes. Stir in half of the Gruyère and the Mimolette. Taste and adjust the seasoning with salt, if needed. Pour the sauce over the cauliflower in the baking dish. Sprinkle with the remaining Gruyère.

Bake until the top is golden and the sauce is bubbling around the edges, about 20 minutes. Serve hot.

try different cheeses
Smoked Gouda and aged Gouda, or goat's milk Cheddar and Manchego

desserts

I have learned from my French friends
and neighbors that simple, seasonal farmhouse desserts
are usually the best ending to a meal. Cheese often plays
a major role in these modest finales. For example, I like
to sweeten goat cheese, ricotta, or fromage blanc with honey
or sugar and combine it with fresh fruit—blood oranges in
winter, strawberries in spring. For a more elaborate
dish, I bake cheese into a tart or a rustic galette,
or whip up a classic cheesecake.

honey-roasted pears with triple-cream cheese

Pears and cheese were made for each other, and this quick-and-easy dish proves that. Roasting the pears with a little butter and honey, then topping them with a rich and creamy cheese like Brillat-Savarin or Explorateur makes a decadent finish to a fall or winter meal.

4 pears such as Anjou or Bosc, about 1½ lb (750 g) total weight

4 Tbsp (2 oz/60 g) unsalted butter, melted

¼ cup (3 oz/90 g) honey

¼ lb (125 g) triple-cream cheese, cut into 8 slices

Sliced almonds for serving (optional)

Preheat the oven to 400°F (200°C). Cut the pears in half lengthwise, leaving the stem intact on one half, then core them, making a small round cavity (a melon baller works well). Brush the bottom of a baking dish with half of the melted butter and place the pears in it, cut side down. Brush the pears with the remaining melted butter.

Roast until the pears are easily pierced with a fork, about 15 minutes, or up to 30 minutes if the pears were very firm. Turn the pears, brush the cut surface with the honey, and roast for about 5 minutes longer.

Transfer the hot pears to a platter and pour any juices in the pan over them. Place a scoop of triple-cream cheese on each pear half and sprinkle with the almonds, if desired. Serve at once.

serve with wine
A sparkling wine, dessert wine such as *vin santo* or Sauternes, or fragrant white like Gewürztraminer or Viognier

ricotta with blood orange, pistachio, and honey

My husband and I tend almost fifty blood orange trees, and pistachio trees grow nearby. In the winter we host beehives on our orchard, and the beekeeper pays us in honey. So when I make my own ricotta, this is truly a local dessert. You can vary the fruit with the season.

2 blood oranges

½ cup (4 oz/125 g) fresh whole-milk ricotta cheese

½ cup (2 oz/60 g) pistachio nuts, chopped

Pomegranate seeds for garnish (optional)

¼ cup (3 oz/90 g) honey

Using a sharp knife, cut a slice off the top and bottom of 1 blood orange, exposing the flesh. Stand the fruit upright and, following the contour of the fruit, cut down to remove the peel and pith in wide strips. Repeat with the second blood orange. You can segment the fruit or slice it. To segment the fruit, hold it over a bowl in one hand and with the other hand, cut along both sides of each segment to free it from the membrane, letting each segment drop into the bowl. Pick out any seeds with the tip of the knife, then cut the segments in half crosswise. To slice the oranges, cut them crosswise into thin slices, then pick out any seeds with the tip of the knife.

Divide the cheese equally among 4 dessert bowls or short glasses. Divide the oranges among the bowls, arranging them on top of the cheese. Sprinkle evenly with the pistachios and pomegranates, if desired, then drizzle each bowl with 1 tablespoon of the honey and serve at once.

serve with wine

A Bandol-style rosé, a sparkling wine such as prosecco or *cava*, or Sauvignon Blanc

farmstead cheddar and apple galette

Here is my version of the apple pie I ate as a child, which came topped with a thick slice of Cheddar. I use puff pastry for a lighter crust, skip the pan in favor of a free-form galette, and mix tart Granny Smith apples from my backyard with sweet Golden Delicious for depth of flavor.

1 sheet frozen puff pastry, about ½ lb (250 g), thawed according to package instructions

All-purpose flour for dusting

¼ cup (2½ oz/75 g) apricot jam

1½ lb (750 g) apples (about 2 large), peeled, halved, cored, and cut lengthwise into slices ⅛ inch (3 mm) thick

4 Tbsp (2 oz/60 g) sugar

1 Tbsp fresh lemon juice

¼ lb (125 g) farmstead Cheddar cheese, shredded

2 Tbsp whole milk

Unfold the sheet of puff pastry. On a lightly floured work surface, roll it out into a 12-inch (30-cm) square. Using a sharp knife, trim off the corners to make a round about 12 inches (30 cm) in diameter. Lay the round on a sheet of parchment paper and transfer to a baking sheet. Pinch the edges up to form a generous ¼-inch (6-mm) rim. Spread the jam on the pastry and place in the freezer for 10 minutes.

Meanwhile, in a bowl, combine the apple slices, 2 tablespoons of the sugar, and the lemon juice and toss to coat the apples evenly. Remove the pastry from the freezer and sprinkle with the cheese. Arrange the apple slices, overlapping them slightly, in concentric circles on top. Sprinkle the apples with the remaining 2 tablespoons sugar. Brush the edge of the pastry with the milk. Return to the freezer for 10 minutes. Preheat the oven to 375°F (190°C).

Bake the galette until the pastry is puffed and browned and the apples are lightly golden, about 30 minutes. Cover loosely with aluminum foil and let cool for 5 minutes on the baking sheet. Using a long knife, separate the galette from the parchment paper and transfer to a serving plate. Serve warm or at room temperature.

serve with wine
Late-harvest Viognier or Riesling

cheese blintzes with berry compote

Soft, low-fat farmer cheese, sweetened with sugar, is a classic filling for blintzes. It can be loose and crumbly or, if pressed, firm. These little packets take time to prepare but won't disappoint. Add cherry or berry compote, and you'll have a new favorite dessert.

FOR THE BLINTZES

1 cup (5 oz/155 g) all-purpose flour

½ tsp sea salt

3 large eggs

¾ cup (6 fl oz/180 ml) whole milk

3 Tbsp unsalted butter, melted, plus more at room temperature for frying

FOR THE FILLING

1 cup (8 oz/250 g) farmer cheese

1 cup (8 oz/250 g) fresh whole-milk ricotta cheese

2 Tbsp sugar

¼ tsp grated orange zest

½ tsp vanilla extract

4 Tbsp (2 oz/60 g) unsalted butter

Cherry Compote (page 48) or store-bought compote

To make the blintz batter, in a bowl, whisk together the flour and salt. Add the eggs, milk, and ¾ cup (6 fl oz/180 ml) water and whisk until smooth, then whisk in the 3 tablespoons melted butter. Cover and refrigerate for 1 hour. Alternatively, combine the initial ingredients in a food processor and process until smooth, about 4 seconds, then add the melted butter and process to mix. Pour into a bowl, cover, and refrigerate for 20 minutes.

To cook the blintzes, heat a large frying pan over medium heat until a drop of water flicked on the surface sizzles and evaporates. Brush with about ½ teaspoon room-temperature butter, then ladle ¼ cup (2 fl oz/60 ml) batter onto the center. Tilt the pan to cover the bottom evenly. Cook until the edges begin to brown and the top is set, 1½–2 minutes. Turn and cook for about 1 minute longer. Transfer to a plate. Repeat to make about 12 blintzes total, buttering the pan as needed and stacking the finished blintzes with waxed paper between them.

To make the cheese filling, in a bowl, stir together the cheeses, sugar, orange zest, and vanilla until well blended.

To assemble the blintzes, spread a generous 2½ tablespoons of the filling in the center of each blintz. Fold in the sides and then the ends to enclose the filling and form a rectangle. In a large frying pan over medium heat, melt 2 tablespoons of the butter. When the butter sizzles, add half of the blintzes, seam side down, and fry until lightly browned, about 2 minutes. Gently turn and fry the second side until lightly browned, about 2 minutes. Transfer to individual plates. Repeat with the remaining blintzes and butter. Serve hot with the compote.

dried fig and fresh ricotta pudding

SERVES 4–6

Ricotta makes as perfect a dessert as it does a pasta filling. Although this pudding, flavored with cloves and baked in a gingersnap crust, could be served on its own, I like to dress it up with dried figs plumped in a Marsala syrup. Any fig works; I use black Missions from my trees.

Unsalted butter for greasing

1 Tbsp fine
gingersnap crumbs

3 large eggs

2 cups (1 lb/500 g)
fresh whole-milk
ricotta cheese

3 Tbsp sugar

1 tsp ground cloves

⅛ tsp sea salt

8–10 dried figs,
hard stem tips
removed, cut into
quarters lengthwise

1 cup (8 fl oz/250 ml)
sweet Marsala

Preheat the oven to 375°F (190°C). Butter a 9-inch (23-cm) pie pan. Sprinkle the prepared pan with the gingersnap crumbs, shaking the pan to distribute them evenly.

In a blender or food processor, combine the eggs, cheese, sugar, cloves, and salt and process until smooth. Pour into the prepared pie pan. Bake until slightly puffed and lightly golden, about 25 minutes. Let cool completely on a rack.

In a saucepan, combine the figs and Marsala. Let stand for 10 minutes, then place the pan over medium heat, bring to a simmer, and cook until the figs have softened, about 10 minutes.

To serve, cut the pudding into wedges and divide among 4–6 dessert plates. Spoon the warm figs and their liquid over each serving.

serve with wine
A high-acid white such as a dry Riesling or Sauvignon Blanc

roasted pecorino with honey and nuts

SERVES 6

Warm, melted, and gooey, baked pecorino makes for a distinctive take on the after-dinner cheese plate. A drizzle of golden honey plays sweet against the saltiness of the cheese, and a handful of fragrant toasted walnuts makes this simple dessert sublime. Serve with crusty bread.

½ cup (2 oz/60 g) walnut halves

½ lb (250 g) pecorino cheese

¼ cup (3 oz/90 g) honey

Preheat the oven to 350°F (180°C). Spread the walnuts in a single layer in a pie pan or small rimmed baking sheet. Toast, stirring occasionally, until the nuts are fragrant and lightly browned, about 10 minutes. Remove from the oven and set aside.

Meanwhile, cut the cheese into slices ¼ inch (6 mm) thick and arrange overlapping in a small baking dish. Bake until the cheese melts and starts to turn golden, about 10 minutes.

Remove the baking dish from the oven, scatter the walnuts over the top of the pecorino, and drizzle with the honey. Serve warm.

try different cheeses
Parmigiano-Reggiano or *grana padano*

serve with wine or liqueur
A dessert wine such as *vin santo* or muscat, a dry sherry like Manzanilla, a medium-bodied red such as Chianti, or a digestif on ice such as Cynar or Ramazzotti

plum tartlets with ginger and chèvre

SERVES 6

These tartlets, with a not-too-sweet cheese base, juicy fruit, and crunchy crust, are so good that even my husband, Jim, who eschews desserts, eats them with relish. You can use nectarines, peaches, or thinly sliced apples in place of the plums. Serve each with a scoop of ice cream or gelato.

1 sheet (½ package) frozen puff pastry, thawed according to package directions

All-purpose flour for dusting

¼ lb (125 g) soft goat cheese

½ cup (4 oz/125 g) plus 1–2 Tbsp sugar

1 large egg

½ cup (4 fl oz/125 ml) heavy cream

2 tsp minced crystallized ginger

¼ tsp ground ginger

3–4 plums, pitted and cut into slices ¼ inch (6 mm) thick

Preheat the oven to 375°F (190°C). Line a baking sheet with parchment paper. Unfold the sheet of puff pastry. On a lightly floured work surface, roll it out into a 9-by-13-inch (23-by-33-cm) rectangle about ⅛ inch (3 mm) thick. Use a pastry cutter to cut the pastry into 6 squares, about 3½ inches (9 cm) each. Transfer the squares to the prepared baking sheet. Pinch the edges up to form a generous ½-inch (12-mm) rim. Place the pastry in the freezer for 15 minutes.

In a bowl, whisk together the cheese, ½ cup sugar, egg, cream, crystallized ginger, and ground ginger to form a smooth paste. Spread evenly over the bottom of the pastry squares. Arrange the plum slices in an attractive pattern on top. Sprinkle 1–2 tablespoons sugar evenly over the plums.

Bake until the pastry is puffed and browned and the plums are soft and slightly golden, about 30 minutes. Cover loosely with aluminum foil and let cool for 10 minutes. Using a spatula, transfer the tartlets to individual plates. Serve warm.

serve with wine
A bright and lively white such as Sancerre or Grüner Veltliner

mascarpone, almond, and apricot crostata

When apricots are ripe and at their peak, I use them as much as possible, from making ice cream to preparing this chilled *crostata*. The cheeses are combined into a thick cream filling, then poured into the almond crust, chilled, and topped with the fresh fruit and nuts.

FOR THE CRUST

½ cup (2½ oz/75 g) blanched almonds

½ cup (4 oz/125 g) unsalted butter

1 cup (5 oz/155 g) all-purpose flour

¼ cup (2 oz/60 g) sugar

FOR THE FILLING

6 oz (185 g) cream cheese, softened

1 cup (8 oz/250 g) mascarpone

¼ cup (2 oz/60 g) crème fraîche

¼ cup (2 oz/60 g) sugar

¼ tsp almond extract

6–8 apricots, pitted and thinly sliced

½ cup (5 oz/155 g) apricot preserves, puréed and heated until warm

¼ cup (1½ oz/45 g) slivered almonds, toasted

To make the crust, in a food processor or blender, finely chop the almonds until they look like coarse bread crumbs. In a large frying pan over medium-high heat, melt the butter. When it foams, add the flour, sugar, and almonds and cook, stirring occasionally, until the mixture is lightly golden and crumbly, 3–4 minutes. Let the mixture cool until it can be handled, then press it into the bottom and up the sides of a 9-inch (23-cm) tart pan with a removable bottom. Refrigerate for at least 2 hours or up to overnight.

To make the filling, in bowl, using an electric mixer, beat together the cream cheese, mascarpone, crème fraîche, sugar, and almond extract until smooth. Spread into the chilled crust. Cover and refrigerate the cheese filling overnight.

Just before serving, remove the tart from the pan and place on a serving plate. Arrange the apricot slices, slightly overlapping, in concentric circles over the cheese filling. Brush the apricot slices with the warmed preserves to glaze them. Sprinkle with the almonds and serve at once.

serve with wine
A sparkling wine such as prosecco or *cava*, or a chilled rosé

chocolate cupcakes with fromage blanc swirls

These light, ethereal cupcakes are easy to make and not too sweet. Small children, including my granddaughter Oona, love to do the swirling part. The *fromage blanc* adds a wonderful creaminess to the batter, and a savory tang and visual intrigue to the finished cupcake.

FOR THE SWIRL

¼ cup (2 oz/60 g) sugar

2 Tbsp butter,
at room temperature

1 large egg

1 Tbsp all-purpose flour

⅔ cup (5 oz/155 g)
fromage blanc

FOR THE BATTER

1¾ cups (9 oz/280 g)
all-purpose flour

1¼ cups (10 oz/315 g)
sugar

1 tsp baking soda

½ tsp salt

1 cup (8 oz/250 g)
sour cream

6 Tbsp (3 oz/90 g) butter,
at room temperature, cut
into ½-inch (12-mm) pieces

1 tsp vanilla extract

3 oz (90 g) 70 percent
cacao bittersweet chocolate,
coarsely chopped

2 large eggs

Preheat the oven to 350°F (180°C). Line 24 standard muffin cups with paper liners. To make the swirl, in a bowl, beat together the sugar and butter until smooth. Beat in the egg until incorporated, then add the flour and *fromage blanc* and again beat until smooth. Set aside.

To make the batter, in a bowl, whisk together the flour, sugar, baking soda, and salt. In a second bowl, beat together the sour cream, butter, and vanilla until smooth. Place the chocolate in a heatproof bowl over (but not touching) simmering water in a saucepan and stir until melted and smooth. Let cool, 1–2 minutes. Add the sour cream mixture, eggs, and ¼ cup (2 fl oz/60 ml) hot water to the flour mixture and beat just until smooth, then beat in the chocolate until incorporated.

Spoon the batter into the muffin cups, filling each two-thirds to three-fourths full and reserving about ½ cup (4 fl oz/125 ml) of the batter. Top each cup with a generous tablespoon of the cheese swirl mixture. Using a knife, dip into the chocolate batter under the cheese mixture, bring a bit up, and twist it into a swirl. Then dot the top of each cup with about 1 teaspoon of the reserved ½ cup batter and twist again. Bake the cupcakes until puffed and a toothpick inserted into the middle comes out clean, 15–20 minutes. Let cool completely on a rack before removing from the muffin cups.

---

try different cheeses
Fresh whole-milk ricotta or mascarpone

lemon cheesecake

Be sure to use whole-milk ricotta for this airy, Italian-style cheesecake. This is a favorite dessert at my house over the winter holidays, and I make it with the Meyer lemons that grow just outside my kitchen door. Lisbon or Eureka lemons work, too, and impart a little more tartness.

FOR THE CRUST

6 oz (185 g) gingersnaps, plus more if needed

1¼ cups (5 oz/155 g) walnut halves

¼ cup (2 oz/60 g) sugar

5 Tbsp (2½ oz/75 g) unsalted butter, or as needed, melted

FOR THE FILLING

½ lb (250 g) cream cheese, at room temperature

1 cup (8 oz/250 g) fresh whole-milk ricotta cheese

1 cup (8 oz/250 g) sugar

4 large eggs, separated, at room temperature

⅔ cup (5 fl oz/160 ml) heavy cream

Finely grated zest of 2 lemons, plus ¼ cup (2 fl oz/65 ml) fresh lemon juice

1 tsp pure vanilla extract

⅛ tsp salt

Confectioners' sugar for dusting (optional)

To make the crust, preheat the oven to 325°F (165°C). In a food processor, pulse the gingersnaps until finely ground. Transfer to a bowl. Add the walnuts to the work bowl, process until finely ground, and add to the cookie crumbs. (Alternatively, for a nut-free crust, omit the walnuts and add an additional 4 oz/60 g of gingersnaps.) Add the sugar and 5 tablespoons melted butter and mix well, adding more butter if the crumbs don't cling together. Transfer to a 9-inch (23-cm) springform pan and press over the bottom and 1½ inches (4 cm) up the sides (it is fine if the edges are uneven). Bake until lightly browned, 8–10 minutes. Let cool, then place in the freezer until ready to use.

Reduce the oven temperature to 300°F (150°C). To make the filling, in the clean food processor, combine the cream cheese, ricotta, sugar, egg yolks, cream, lemon zest and juice, vanilla, and salt and process until creamy, 4–5 minutes. Pour into a large bowl. In a separate bowl, using an electric mixer, beat the egg whites until stiff peaks form. Using a rubber spatula, gently fold the whites into the cheese mixture just until combined. Pour the mixture into the reserved chilled crust, smoothing the top.

Place the pan on a foil-lined baking sheet and bake for 30 minutes. Raise the oven temperature to 325°F (165°C) and bake until golden brown on top, the edges are firm, and the center still jiggles, 30–35 minutes. Turn off the oven, open the door, and leave the cake in the oven for about 3 hours (the center will fall slightly). Cover tightly with plastic wrap (do not let the wrap touch the surface) and refrigerate for at least 4 hours or up to 24 hours. To unmold, run a knife around the sides of the cake to loosen them from the pan, then remove the pan sides. If desired, dust the top with confectioners' sugar. Serve cut into wedges, dipping a knife into hot water and wiping it dry before each cut.

red wine–poached pears with gorgonzola

Plump nuggets of creamy Gorgonzola and crisp, earthy walnuts strewn over wine-soaked pears make an understated, sophisticated dessert. I like to serve the pears with plain biscotti, both for dipping into the juice and for spreading with the cheese, and glasses of sherry.

4 ripe but firm pears such as Bosc or Anjou, about 1½ lb (750 g) total weight

1½ cups (12 fl oz/375 ml) dry red wine such as Merlot or Pinot Noir

2 Tbsp sugar

¼ lb (125 g) soft Gorgonzola cheese

1 cup (4 oz/125 g) walnut halves, left whole or coarsely chopped

Cut the pears in half lengthwise, leaving the stem intact on one half, then core them, making a small round cavity (a melon baller works well). Cut out the string that runs down the center from the stem to the cavity. Halve or quarter the pear halves lengthwise, or slice thinly.

In a frying pan or saucepan large enough to hold the pears in a single layer, combine the wine and 2 tablespoons sugar. Bring to a boil over medium heat, stirring to dissolve the sugar. Raise the heat to high and cook until a thin syrup forms, 3–4 minutes. Reduce the heat to low, add the pears, and poach, turning the pears several times, until they are just tender, 15–20 minutes. Be careful not to overcook the pears or they will be mushy.

Transfer the pears and poaching liquid to a nonreactive bowl and let stand for several hours at room temperature, turning the pears occasionally. They will become a deep garnet as they absorb the wine.

To serve, divide the pears among 8 individual plates. Place an equal amount of Gorgonzola on top of each serving, breaking the cheese into pieces, and spoon some of the poaching liquid around the pears. Sprinkle with the walnuts, and serve at once.

serve with wine
A medium-bodied red such as Dolcetto d'Alba, an off-dry sherry, or a late-harvest Sauvignon Blanc

goat cheese and strawberries with mint-balsamic glaze

SERVES 6

I like goat cheese for its flavor and versatility. When I lived in France, I used to make and sell it. Goat cheese can be used for any course from appetizer to dessert and goes well with just about everything, savory or sweet. Whipping some cream into the cheese lightens it.

6 oz (185 g) soft
goat cheese, at room
temperature

¼ cup (2 fl oz/60 ml)
heavy cream

¾ cup (6 oz/185 g) sugar

¼ cup (2 fl oz/60 ml)
balsamic vinegar

2 Tbsp minced fresh mint,
plus finely shredded mint
for garnish

About 1 lb (500 g)
strawberries, halved or
quartered, or sliced if large

In a bowl, using an electric mixer, beat together the cheese, cream, and ¼ cup (2 oz/60 g) of the sugar until the mixture is fluffy. Set aside.

In a saucepan over medium-high heat, combine ½ cup (4 fl oz/125 ml) water and the remaining ½ cup (4 oz/125 g) sugar. Bring to a boil, stirring to dissolve the sugar. Boil until a syrup forms, about 5 minutes. Add the vinegar and continue to boil until a glaze forms that thinly coats the back of a metal spoon, 1–2 minutes longer. Remove from the heat and stir in the minced mint.

To serve, divide the cheese mixture equally among 6 dessert plates or bowls. Spoon the strawberries alongside and drizzle them with the syrup. Garnish the cheese mixture with the shredded mint and serve at once.

serve with wine
A sparkling wine such as prosecco or *cava,* or a dry rosé

oven-roasted summer fruits with ricotta-vanilla cream

SERVES 6–8

This is one of the best summer desserts that I know, and it couldn't be simpler. A spoonful of the roasted fruit, slightly caramelized, is like eating a cobbler without the crust. Ricotta drizzled with honey is a subtle and sublime addition, adding a lush creaminess to the dish.

1 cup (8 oz/250 g) fresh whole-milk ricotta cheese

¼ cup (2 oz/60 g) crème fraîche

½ tsp vanilla extract

6 Tbsp (3 oz/90 g) sugar

2 peaches

2 nectarines

3 plums

8 fresh figs

About ½ lb (250 g) cherries (optional)

1 Tbsp extra-virgin olive oil

Honey for serving

Preheat the oven to 475°F (245°C). In a bowl, combine the cheese, crème fraîche, vanilla, and 2 tablespoons of the sugar and mix well. Cover and refrigerate until ready to use.

Halve the peaches, nectarines, and plums and remove the pits. Cut the halves in half again, if desired. Trim off the hard tip of each fig stem and leave the figs whole. Leave the cherries whole, if using. Combine all the fruits in a roasting pan large enough to fit them in a single layer, drizzle with the olive oil, and turn the fruits several times. Sprinkle with the remaining 4 tablespoons (2 oz/60 g) sugar and turn once or twice.

Roast until the fruits are slightly collapsed and golden or lightly charred, 15–20 minutes.

To serve, spoon the fruits and their cooking juices into a serving bowl or individual dessert bowls. (If you like, halve or quarter the figs lengthwise. If you have used the cherries, let your guests know the pits are intact.) Divide the ricotta mixture among small bowls and swirl a little honey into each serving. Place the ricotta alongside the fruit and serve at once.

serve with wine
A *vinho verde* or Sancerre for white, or a rosé

cheese tools

Box grater-shredder
An indispensable kitchen tool, this stainless-steel box gives the cook the option of four to six different cutting surfaces on each side. They typically include small, pointed rasps for grating, medium and large holes for shredding, and wide slits for shaving. The options accommodate a wide range of cheeses, from shredding semifirm Gruyère to finely grating well-aged pecorino.

Cheese boards
Natural materials are ideal for serving cheese, not only because their appearance complements well-crafted artisanal cheeses, but also because they can withstand moderate slicing and scraping. A wooden board is always a good choice. Marble is another classic option: it will echo the showy veins of a blue and will keep your cheeses slightly cool at the same time. Slate is a material that is gaining popularity. You can write the names of cheeses directly on it in chalk, for an informative and handsome presentation.

Cheese knives
Often sold as part of serving sets, cheese knives and spreaders vary in shape according to the type and style of cheese for which they were designed.

Cleavers A modest-sized version of a butcher's cleaver is an asset on a cheese plate, its sharp, wide blade ideal for cutting semifirm cheeses like Havarti or Gouda into even slices. Small, sharp knives that resemble scrapers are also in the cleaver family, and are especially handy for slicing firm wedges (hold the handle upright for the best cutting action).

Fork-tipped knives A knife with two prongs at the tip is perhaps the most ubiquitous cheese knife. It combines two capabilities, cutting and serving, allowing guests to slice and transfer the fruits of their labor with the same implement. Fork-tipped knives work well with nearly all types of cheese. Separate cheese forks (without a cutting blade) are also sometimes included in sets.

Hard cheese knives Sometimes called Parmesan knives, these stocky knives are designed for cutting into firm, aged cheeses and thus are necessarily sharper and sturdier. They feature triangular- or leaf-shaped blades with pointed, piercing tips.

Soft cheese knives Knives for soft-ripened cheeses typically try to minimize surface area, to prevent oozy, triple creams, like Explorateur, from sticking to the blade. They can be quite slim, and newer designs feature open holes in the blade, to reduce sticking further.

Spreaders Spreaders do exactly as their name implies. Blunt like a butter knife, but with a more rounded, ample tip, these tools evenly spread creamy, luscious cheeses such as chevrès.

Cheese planes
A cheese plane resembles a small, wedge-shaped spatula or cake server. A sharp slit at the base shaves off thin slices when passed over a block of cheese in smooth strokes. Planes should be reserved for use on semifirm and firm cheeses; softer varieties won't pass through the opening as readily.

Rasp graters
This handheld tool was originally developed for woodworking, but quickly found its place in the kitchen as a way to make short work of grating hard cheeses, such as Parmigiano-Reggiano. Rasp graters typically have a handle at one end, and are either long and narrow or paddle shaped. The rasps come in a variety of different cutting surfaces and hole sizes; some include exchangeable blades for more versatility.

Wire slicers
Wire easily cuts through firm cheeses, yielding uniform slices of Jack or Cheddar, for instance, ideal for building sandwiches. Forms vary from simple handheld gadgets resembling vegetable peelers to more sophisticated standing board attachments. For the latter, an arm lowers the wire down through a block of cheese. There are also wire "guillotines," which slide a wire down onto a block from directly above.

cheese terms

Affinage

The craft of aging cheese, which is held as one of the most critical stages in cheese making. An *affineur* is the person who cares for the cheeses as they age. Some makers send their cheeses to specialized *affineurs* for finishing.

Annatto

A natural food coloring made from the red seeds of the achiote tree, annatto is used to color many cheeses, such as Cheddar or Red Leicester, yellow-orange.

AOC

AOC, or *Appellation d'Origin Contrôlée,* is the French regulation system for wines, cheeses, and other agricultural products that grants them regional protection. For example, for a cheese to be officially named Roquefort, it must be aged in the caves of Roquefort-su-Soulzon according to a specific set of standards. DOP, or *Denominazione d'Origine Protetta,* is the Italian equivalent, and DO, or *Denominación de Origen*, is the Spanish equivalent, though no other system is as comprehensive as the French AOC.

Aging

Also called ripening or curing, aging is the process of holding cheeses in a controlled environment so that they develop flavor and texture. In general, the longer a cheese ages, the more whey (moisture) it loses, which means it becomes firmer, drier, and more flavorful.

Artisanal (also see page 8)

The antithesis of mass production, the term *artisanal* describes locally based, small-batch cheese making. It conveys craftsmanship, a respect for raw materials, and a sense of place and seasonality.

Bacteria

The single-cell microorganisms that exist everywhere are an essential element in cheese making. They affect aging, flavor development, and mold growth on rinds. Makers encourage the growth of particular types of bacteria on the surface of various cheeses, to produce bloomy-rind or washed-rind cheeses.

Bloomy Rind

Bloom is the soft mold growth on the exterior of a cheese. A bloomy-rind cheese is a cheese that has an edible rind covered with a flavor-producing mold.

Blue

A cheese with an internal mold, usually blue or green and typically spread throughout the interior. Stilton and Gorgonzola are two of the best-known blue cheeses.

Cave

An underground room or cellar used for aging cheese. Originally, cheeses were aged in natural caves, but nowadays, caves are more often rooms outfitted with humidity and temperature controls.

Clothbound

A cheese that is wrapped in cloth throughout aging, such as many artisanal Cheddars. Unlike wax or plastic, cloth allows the cheese to breathe, which helps in the formation of a natural rind and a deep flavor.

Curds

When milk separates, the solids are known as curds and the liquid is known as whey. The formation of curds is the first step in most cheese making. Some curds are eaten fresh, such as ricotta cheese; others are drained and pressed, resulting in firmer cheeses. If curds are cut and then pressed, the result is a firm, smooth texture. Curds that are "cooked" before they are pressed yield the hardest cheeses, such as Parmigiano-Reggiano. *See also* Stretched Curd.

Double Cream

Fresh or soft-ripened cheeses made with cream in addition to milk are designated double cream or triple cream. Double-cream cheeses must contain at least 60 percent butterfat. *See also* Triple Cream.

Eyes

The holes in the interior of a cheese, such as Swiss, Jarlsberg, Emmentaler, or Havarti. Eyes are caused by the creation of gas during fermentation, which is then released as the cheese ages.

Farmstead (also see page 8)
A term used for cheeses that are made on a farm from the milk of animals raised on the same farm.

Fermentation
A chemical change that happens in various types of food; in dairy, it refers to the process by which bacteria converts lactose to lactic acid. Sour cream, yogurt, and cheese all undergo fermentation.

Fromagier
The traditional French term for a cheese maker, as opposed to a *fromager*, who is a purveyor of cheese or a cheese merchant.

Mold
Molds are the result of fungi growing on foods. Beneficial edible molds are key to the successful production of certain cheeses. Spores are introduced to the surface or the interior of cheeses such as Roquefort or Camembert, adding flavor and texture. Surface molds ripen inward; internal molds ripen throughout the paste.

Natural Rind
A rind that forms naturally on the exterior of a cheese, without the use of aging or other types of agents.

Paste
The interior part of a cheese, as opposed to the rind.

Pasteurization (also see page 15)
The process by which raw milk is heated to a level high enough to kill harmful bacteria. Unfortunately, some good bacteria are also killed in the process, so raw milk cheeses tend to have a more complex flavor.

Penicillium
The primary genus of various fungi used to generate a bloomy rind on some cheeses (*P. candidum*), such as Brie, or to encourage interior veining in other cheeses (*P. roquefortii*), such as Roquefort.

Pressing (also see page 13)
Some cheeses are pressed during aging, to push out more moisture (whey). The result is a drier, firmer cheese. The hardest cheeses are pressed and aged over the longest periods of time.

Raw milk
Milk of any type that has not been pasteurized. *See also* Pasteurization.

Rennet
An extract that causes milk to coagulate or curds to separate from whey. Rennet comes from the stomachs of calves, sheep, or goats. (One legend claims that cheese was invented by an Arab who tried to carry milk across a desert in a container made from an animal's stomach, only to discover that the milk became an edible solid.) Nowadays, plant-based rennet is also used.

Rind
The exterior surface of a cheese, as opposed to the paste. Many rinds are edible. Cheeses covered in wax or wrapped in other materials will not develop a rind, nor will fresh cheeses, which have not had time to grow one.

Stretched Curd
A stretchy, stringlike texture in some cheeses comes from stretching or kneading the fresh curds while they are warm. Depending on type, these stretched-curd cheeses will then be eaten fresh, such as mozzarella, or aged, such as provolone.

Terroir
Literally "land," the term is used to describe the unique role that a particular place and its immediate natural elements play in determining the character of a cheese. Climate, soil, topography, minerals, ground crops, and even the contentment of the animals are all factors. Factory-made cheeses are necessarily excluded; only a cheese that exhibits the place in which it was made is said to have terroir.

Triple Cream
Cheese that contains more than 75 percent butterfat. *See also* Double Cream.

Washed Rind
Term used to describe a cheese that is regularly bathed in water, brine, wine, brandy, oil, or other liquid. These baths keep the rind moist and encourage the growth of beneficial reddish orange bacteria.

Whey
The liquid left behind when milk separates into curds. *See also* Curds.

serving accompaniments

Bread, crackers, and pastries
You can serve nearly any type of bread or cracker with cheese. Baguette slices are a natural with most cheeses, from a pungent washed-rind Muenster to a soft chèvre to a crumbly Cheddar. Chunks of rustic country loaves or torn pieces of focaccia will also work with most cheeses. Crostini, either homemade or store-bought, are good choices for any soft cheese.
Baguette, country, or focaccia for breads; breadsticks; herbed or plain crostini; seeded, water, or whole-grain crackers; biscuits, scones, or fig-walnut cake for pastries

Cured meats
Cured meats are a particularly good match for hard and semifirm cheeses, like Cheddar, Parmesan, and pecorino, but are also tasty with soft and fresh cheeses. Put together a cheese and charcuterie plate or pair a singular cheese and meat from the same region or country, such as mozzarella with prosciutto or Manchego with *serrano* ham.
Bayonne ham, coppa, prosciutto, salami, lomo, jamón ibérico, jamón serrano

Dried fruits
More robustly flavored than fresh fruits, dried fruits add flavor and a pleasantly chewy texture to cheese plates. Dried stone fruits, such as apricots, nectarines, or peaches, are delicious with Cheddars; dates are a good fit with grana padano or pecorino; and figs pair nicely with blues and goat cheeses.
Apples, apricots, cherries, cranberries, dates (Medjool), figs (Smyrna, Calimyrna), nectarines, raisins

Fresh fruits
Seasonal fruits, whole, halved, or cut into wedges or slices, are an excellent way to add a fresh element to any cheese plate. Grapes are a standard accompaniment, but don't shy away from choosing any fruit any time of the year, such as citrus in winter, cherries in spring, stone fruits in summer, and figs, apples, and pears in fall.
Apples, berries, cherries, clementines, figs, grapes, kumquats, nectarines, peaches, pears, plums, pomegranates, tangerines

Fresh vegetables
Delivering crunch, flavor, and often some welcome moisture, fresh vegetables are a good addition to most cheese plates. Select a single seasonal element, such as spring radishes or summer tomatoes, cut them into wedges, and sprinkle them with flaky sea salt, or serve a variety of crudités. Pair with one or more cheeses of nearly any type.
Asparagus, broccoli, carrots, cauliflower, celery, fennel, jicama, radishes, sugar snap peas, tomatoes (heirloom, cherry)

Nuts
Crunchy and earthy, nuts pair well with most cheeses and with sweet or savory accompaniments such as honey, tapenade, fruit preserves, and olives. Serve them blanched, toasted, or spiced with herbs and salt (page 40). For a delicious sweet-and-savory pairing, serve sugared nuts alongside blue cheese.
Almonds, hazelnuts, pecans, pistachios, walnuts

Olives
Meaty and briny, olives are natural mates for almost any cheese, from feta to Parmesan, mozzarella to Cheddar, and can be paired with other savory accompaniments, such as nuts or charcuterie. For a good Spanish-inspired match, serve Warm Citrus Olives (page 37) with any Spanish cheese, such as Garrotxa or Manchego; for an Italian offering, serve oil-cured olives with a pecorino.
Bella di Cerignola, Gaeta, Kalamata, Manzanilla, Niçoise, Picholine, Sicilian

Preserves and spreads
Savory tapenade and sweet fruit butters, jams, and marmalades are delicious spread directly on pieces of hard cheese or layered with soft cheeses on a baguette slice or cracker. Combinations include pickled vegetables with Cheddar, honeycomb with Gorgonzola, or quince paste with Manchego.
Candied citrus peel, chutneys, compotes, fig paste, fruit preserves, honey, honeycomb, jams, marmalades, quince paste (membrillo), pickled vegetables, tapenade

know your cheeses

Abbaye de Belloc
semifirm I sheep's milk I France
Invented by Benedictine monks, this ivory-colored cheese with a brownish rind has a dense, creamy texture and burnt caramel flavor.

Abondance
semifirm I cow's milk I France
Sharing a name with both the commune in which it originated and the breed of cattle from whose milk it is exclusively made, pale yellow, buttery Abondance is pressed in large rounds that develop a light brown rind. It is sometimes categorized as hard, though it is not a grating cheese.

Appenzeller
semifirm I cow's milk I Switzerland
Smooth, dense, and complex, straw-colored Appenzeller is a pressed cheese with a long monastic history. A thin, blue-gray or brownish line beneath the rind shows evidence of multiple baths in an herbal brine. It is sold at three different stages of aging: after three to four months, four to six months, and six months or longer.

Ardrahan
semifirm I cow's milk I Ireland
A full-flavored, semifirm farmstead cheese made with vegetable rennet. Made in Cork County, Ireland, it is exported by London's famous Neal's Yard Dairy.

Asiago
semifirm, hard I cow's milk I Italy
Young Asiago is made from whole cow's milk and has an elastic texture and a sweet, mild flavor and aroma. The aged version, made from skim milk and left to cure for up to two years, has a grainy texture and a sharper, yet fruity flavor.

Banon
natural-rind I cow's, goat's, sheep's milk I France
A specialty of Haute-Provence, this small, round AOC cheese, aged just two weeks, is moist, nutty, and pleasantly pungent. It is easily recognizable by its chestnut-leaf wrapping, which imparts wood and fruit flavors to the cheese.

Basajo
blue I sheep's milk I Italy
Residents of the Veneto insist that this wine-soaked blue originated at the end of World War I, when a farmer hid his cheeses in a wine barrel to avoid confiscation by hungry troops. More likely, however, velvety, creamy, mellow Basajo is part of the long Italian tradition of aging cheeses in grape must.

Beaufort
hard I cow's milk I France
An alpine cheese made in the Comté (Gruyère) style, buttery Beaufort is a good melting cheese and a popular choice for fondue. It is smooth textured and fruity, but with a sharper flavor than Gruyère.

Bethmale Vache
washed-rind I cow's milk I France
Made from raw cow's milk in the Midi-Pyrénées, this pungent, semifirm cheese has a lush buttery, mushroomy flavor.

Bleu d'Auvergne
blue I cow's milk I France
A crusty reddish orange rind conceals a firm yet creamy interior with irregular threads of blue-gray mold—the same type used to make beloved Roquefort. This blue is younger and milder than Roquefort, however, with a sharp clean taste and creamier texture.

Boursin
fresh I cow's milk I France
Boursin is easy to love, which means some connoisseurs disdain it. Originating in Normandy, it is mild, sold plain or flavored—garlic and herbs, pepper, or shallot and chive—and the texture ranges from moist and crumbly to firm and smooth.

Brescianella Stagionata
semisoft I cow's milk I Italy
This square gem from Lombardy has a wrinkly orange rind that conceals an oozing, creamy, pungent cheese.

Brie
soft-ripened | cow's milk | France

The King of Cheeses, Brie has been enjoyed for centuries in its native Île-de-France. Mass-produced Brie is a bland, disappointing echo of the real thing, which is made from unpasteurized milk and is aged for less than sixty days, making it unavailable in the United States. Ripe Brie has a smooth, not-quite-runny texture, a dry, cracked white rind, and a mushroomy flavor. An overripe wheel reeks of ammonia.

Brillat-Savarin
soft-ripened | cow's milk | France

The famous dairy cows of Normandy contribute their rich and flavorful milk to create this triple-cream cheese, buttery and smooth, with a thick, soft white crust. The longer it ages, the richer and tangier its flavor.

Brin d'Amour
semisoft | sheep's milk | France

This Corsican contribution to the cheese plate is a unique herb-dusted specimen, gleaning flavor from such herbs as rosemary, savory, and thyme. It is served either young and lush or slightly aged and firm.

Burrata
fresh | cow's, water buffalo's milk | Italy

A ball of fresh mozzarella stuffed with a luscious blend of unfinished mozzarella curd and cream, burrata is sweet and earthy, with just a hint of sourness. It was first crafted in Puglia in the 1920s. Today, lesser versions are made in and outside Italy from cow's milk.

Cabrales
blue | cow's, goat's, sheep's milk | Spain

Aged in limestone caves near the sea in Asturias, this much-admired compact, creamy cheese with irregular veins of blue-green mold is made from cow's milk or a blend of cow's and goat's or sheep's milk, depending on the season.

Camembert
soft-ripened | cow's milk | France

Brie's kissing cousin, Camembert hails from Normandy and features a similar powdery white rind, rich and creamy interior, and meaty, wild mushroom flavor. Some reddish brown on the white rind is a good sign; a pure white, velvety rind means the cheese is not yet fully ripe. A strong ammonia odor signals it is overripe.

Cantal
semifirm | cow's milk | France

A well-regarded cheese of Auvergne, Cantal is moist and elastic, with a milky aroma and pleasant tang, when young. As it ages, it becomes more like a fine Cheddar, nutty with an acidic finish.

Cashel blue
blue | cow's milk | Ireland

This firm, crumbly artisanal blue has a fresh, slightly sharp flavor. Cashel mellows and becomes creamier with age, and collapses on itself when it is perfectly ripe.

Chaource
soft-ripened | cow's milk | France

This white, bloomy-rind cheese from the Champagne region has a grainy texture. Tart when young, it mellows to a still sharp but also earthy mushroom flavor as it ages.

Chaumes
washed-rind | cow's, goat's milk | France

Made in Périgord, this rich, creamy cheese has a deep orange rind typical of washed-rind cheeses. However, it is milder than some of its cousins, making it a good starting point for exploring the cheese category.

Cheddar
semifirm | cow's milk | England

A handcrafted, well-aged Cheddar is one of the world's great cheeses: a firm yet yielding texture, a fresh aroma, and a nutty, savory, sweet yet tart flavor with a lingering finish. Cheddars from the British Isles (exported by Neal's Yard Dairy) and artisanal Cheddars from Vermont or California are generally first-rate.

Cheshire
semifirm | cow's milk | England

One of England's oldest cheeses, Cheshire has a mildly salty taste and a moist, crumbly, dense texture. As with Cheddar, artisanal brands are far superior to their mass-produced counterparts.

Chèvre
fresh | goat's milk | France

Smooth, tart, and earthy yet mild, fresh goat's milk cheese is an icon of France, especially in the Loire Valley and Poitou regions. Young chèvre, with its lemony flavor, is wonderful spread on a baguette or crumbled on a salad. Longer-aged chèvres, such as chèvre d'or, are firm enough to slice. Laura Chenel pioneered the production of high-quality chèvre in America in the 1970s.

Chèvrefeuille

natural-rind I goat's milk I France

Like many of the foodstuffs that come out of Périgord, this cheese, with its pure white interior and gently tart flavor, is loaded with character. Fashioned in a variety of shapes, it is sometimes sold plain and other times sprinkled with herbs and peppercorns.

Colby

semifirm (washed-curd) I cow's milk I US

The sweet, buttery, mild flavor of this Wisconsin cheese is reminiscent of a young Cheddar.

Comté

hard I cow's milk I France

Made in the alpine area of eastern France, Gruyère de Comté, generally known as Comté (and pronounced as if the *m* were an *n*), is a type of Gruyère with a fruity, nutty flavor and long, spicy finish.

Cream Cheese

fresh I cow's milk I worldwide

Where would bagels and lox be without cream cheese? Smooth, creamy, and mild, this versatile cheese, made from light or heavy cream, is also an important ingredient in dessert baking.

Crescenza

fresh I cow's milk I Italy

This white, rindless cheese, which originated in northern Italy—the best comes from near Milan—has a creamy, luscious, mild flavor and a runny, almost liquid consistency at room temperature.

Crottin de Chavignol

natural-rind I goat's milk I France

Much-imitated, this crottin is one of the classic and most famous goat cheeses of the Loire Valley. Formed into small disks, Crottin de Chavignol has a nutty, rich flavor and is eaten at various stages of maturation. When young, it is white, soft, solid, mildly tangy, and has a thin rind. Aged cheeses have a yellow, crumbly, sharply flavored interior and a dark, thick rind.

Cusiè in Foglie di Castagne

semifirm I cow's milk I Italy

Made from the milk of cows and goats pastured all summer in the Piedmont, Cusiè is aged for eighteen to twenty-four months, then wrapped in chestnut leaves (*foglie di castagne*) to add a distinctive nutty flavor.

Danish blue

blue I cow's milk I Denmark

Created in the twentieth century as a cheaper alternative to Roquefort, this mass-produced blue is sharp, salty, and robust, with a creamy consistency.

Derby

semifirm I cow's milk I England

Plain Derby is buttery and golden and has a mellow, Cheddar-like flavor. But when it is laced with an herb—most commonly sage—it becomes a strikingly marbled creation with emerald veins running throughout.

Edam

semifirm (washed-curd) I cow's milk I Holland

Mild, smooth, and with little aroma, this wildly popular Dutch cheese has a straw-hued interior and a yellow, red, or black wax coating (black wax indicates longer aging).

Emmentaler

semifirm I cow's milk I Switzerland

Golden yellow Emmentaler has the classic "holey" texture of Swiss cheese. Its longer aging (a minimum of four months), customary with mountain cheeses, gives it a floral aroma and fruity taste with tingling acidity.

Époisses de Bourgogne

washed-rind I cow's milk I France

One of the best-known washed-rind cheeses, Époisses was born among the vineyards of Burgundy. Its telltale orange rind is created by washing the cheese with marc (French grappa), resulting in a strong barnyardy odor. A smooth, savory, meaty interior tastes somewhat milder than the cheese smells.

Explorateur

soft-ripened I cow's milk I France

The Île-de-France is the birthplace of this alluring triple cream, with a mushroomy, buttery taste and firm texture.

Farmer Cheese

fresh I cow's milk I worldwide

Made by adding rennet and a bacterial culture to milk, then draining off the whey and pressing the curd to remove moisture, farmer cheese appears in many guises around the world, including as queso fresco in Mexico. It's grainier, less rich, and tangier than cream cheese.

Feta

fresh l cow's, goat's, sheep's milk l Greece

This brined cheese, under both the same and different names, is made in several countries in the Mediterranean and along the Black Sea. A European Union ruling has limited the use of the term *feta* to the Greek cheese, forcing other union members to relabel their products. Salty and savory, with a firm, crumbly texture, Greek feta is made from sheep's (at least 70 percent) and goat's milk. Bulgaria (sheep's and/or goat's milk), Denmark (cow's milk), and France (usually sheep's milk) are also important sources of the cheese.

Fleur du Maquis

semisoft l sheep's milk l France

Literally "flower of the maquis"—the rough, scrubby landscape of the island of Corsica—this luscious, fine-textured cheese is covered with a blue-gray mold and a coating of herbs (rosemary, savory, and juniper).

Fontina

semifirm l cow's milk l Italy

Dense, smooth, and elastic, with an earthy hint of nuts and mushrooms balanced by a fresh acidity, Fontina is an excellent melting cheese. The label is often slapped onto lesser cheeses, so look for Fontina Val d'Aosta, which has been made in Piedmont's Aosta Valley for more than eight centuries.

Fourme d'Ambert

blue l cow's milk l France

Dense like Stilton, this classic blue of Auvergne has a supple, not-too-rich flavor with a nutty finish.

Fromage Frais

fresh l cow's, goat's, sheep's milk l France

This simple fresh cheese, originating in northern France and Belgium, has a mousselike texture and mild citrus flavor. It is often served like plain yogurt, with honey or fresh fruit, for breakfast or dessert.

Gariotin

semisoft l goat's milk l France

These small disks of pale, smooth cheese with a bloomy rind that wrinkles with age, have a pleasant tang and an aroma that reveals the milk from which they are made.

Garrotxa

semifirm l goat's milk l Spain

Named for an area in Catalonia, this pressed cheese has a brownish gray rind, moist white flesh, and milky flavor.

Gjetost

semifirm l goat's, cow's milk l Scandinavia

This unassuming, strong-flavored yet mildly sweet brown paste, sold in little cubes, is known by a different name in each Scandinavian county (brunost, mesost, mysuostur, and myseost, in Norway, Sweden, Iceland, and Denmark, respectively) and by gjetost in the United States. It is made by boiling whey with milk and cream, which produces its unique caramel color and flavor.

Gloucester

semifirm l cow's milk l England

This four-century-old traditional British cheese is named after a breed of cattle. Single Gloucester uses the milk of only one milking; Double Gloucester includes cream from a second milking and is aged longer. Both resemble a crumbly Cheddar. Cotswold is a Double Gloucester with added chives and onions.

Gorgonzola

blue l cow's milk l Italy

One of the world's great cheeses, Gorgonzola has a rough, reddish crust and a white to pale yellow interior with blue-green streaks. Creamier and sweeter than Stilton, its flavor is sharp, spicy, and equally complex. Gorgonzola labeled *dolce* is younger, mild and creamy; *naturale* or *piccante* is firmer and more pungent.

Gorwydd Caerphilly

semisoft l cow's milk l Wales

A regular lunch-box item of generations of Welsh miners, this handcrafted cheese nearly disappeared, until revived by the Trethowan family. Aged for sixty days on the farm, it is snowy white and crumbly at the center and smooth and straw colored closer to its natural rind.

Gouda

semifirm (washed-curd) l cow's milk l Holland

When young, this popular cheese has a sweet, fruit flavor. As it ages, it grows more savory and complex. Look for a black wax coating for a well-aged version. Distinctive varieties include eighteen-month UnieKaas Reserve Gouda and three-year Saenkanter Gouda, both rich in salty, butterscotch flavor and orange in hue.

Grana Padano

hard l cow's milk l Italy

Similar to Parmigiano-Reggiano, this excellent grating cheese is made in the same general area. Fashioned from partially skim milk and usually aged from one to two years, it is a pale color and has a fresh, fruity flavor.

Gruyère
semifirm | cow's milk | Switzerland
Denser than Emmentaler, Gruyère has a creamy yet slightly grainy texture and a robust, nutty, herbal flavor. Aged for a minimum of five months, it is an excellent cooking cheese, especially good for gratins and fondue.

Halloumi
semisoft | sheep's, goat's milk | Cyprus
This stretched-curd, mildly salty, white cheese is noted for its ability to hold its shape when fried or even grilled, making it a popular ingredient in eastern Mediterranean cooking. Some halloumi is allowed to age until it is quite hard. Mass-produced halloumi contains cow's milk.

Havarti
semisoft | cow's milk | Denmark
Ivory to pale yellow, Havarti has a creamy but slightly spongy texture, thanks to many small holes, and a full-bodied flavor that becomes more pungent with age.

Humboldt Fog
soft-ripened | goat's milk | California
A wedge of this celebrated California cheese looks like a delicious piece of fluffy layer cake: a thin sheet of gray ash separates layers of pure white, mousselike goat cheese and a powdery white rind "frosts" the slice.

Idiazabal
semifirm, hard | sheep's milk | Spain
One of Spain's prized sheep's milk cheeses, Idiazábal has a firm, pale interior and a hard, inedible rind. Buttery and nutty in flavor, it is also sometimes smoked. Longer aging yields a hard cheese ideal for grating.

Jack, Dry
hard | cow's milk | California
Monterey Jack that has been aged for up to two years, yielding a dry, hard cheese with the properties of Parmesan. The creation of Italian immigrants living in California during World War II, as an alternative to Italian grating cheeses. The deep yellow cheese is slightly crunchy, with a sweet, fruity, sharp flavor.

Jarlsberg
semifirm | cow's milk | Norway
This widely known golden yellow cheese, though similar to Switzerland's Emmentaler, is milder and sweeter.

Lancashire
semifirm | cow's milk | England
When traditionally made by combining curds from different days, a stippled texture and particularly complex flavor is the result. Sold young and moist with a mild chive tang, or aged with a more intense onion flavor. Artisanal products, like Mrs Kirkham's Lancashire, have a crumbly texture and robust taste. Mass-produced Lancashire is creamier and blander.

Langres
washed-rind | cow's milk | France
A small, wrinkly cheese from the Champagne region, rich, dense Langres is usually aged for only about five weeks. Unfortunately, because raw-milk cheeses aged for less than sixty days cannot be imported into the United States, shoppers on this side of the Atlantic are left with the less-satisfying pasteurized-milk version.

La Tur
fresh | cow's, goat's, sheep's milk | Italy
Made from a blend of three milks, this rich, buttery cheese from the hilly Piedmont has a paper-thin "skin," a well-balanced flavor, and an exceptionally creamy texture reminiscent of thickened crème fraîche.

Limburger
washed-rind | cow's milk | Germany
The original stinky cheese, Limburger is a semisoft cheese with a pungent odor that carries through to the taste. If you care to brave it, you'll find Limburger is supple, firm, meaty, and spicy. An overripe wheel is unbearable to most people.

Lincolnshire Poacher
hard | cow's milk | England
Invented by cheese makers Simon and Tim Jones in 1992, this nutty, slightly fruity, mildly sweet cheese is a recent addition to the English tradition of pressed cheeses made from raw cow's milk. The cylinders have a slate gray rind and pale interior.

Livarot
washed-rind | cow's milk | France
Native to Normandy, this earthy, pungent cheese is customarily drunk with one of the traditional local beverages, cider or Calvados. The interior is pale gold and the rind is brown-orange, often due to annatto.

Mahón
semifirm | cow's milk | Spain
Mildly salty and pleasantly acidic, this ivory to yellow cheese, with a yellow to orange rind, is made on the island of Minorca, in the Balearics. It is eaten both young, when milky, and aged, when it turns piquant.

Manchego
semifirm, hard | sheep's milk | Spain
The thick, creamy sheep's milk of La Mancha is used to make this ivory-colored cheese with a brownish rind. Young Manchego is mild and creamy; when left to cure for more than three months, it is labeled *viejo* (aged) and is dry and firm yet rich on the tongue, with a nutty, caramel, peppery finish.

Mascarpone
fresh | cow's milk | Italy
Mild with a pleasant acidic bite, thick, velvety texture, and a richness that makes it a common ingredient for desserts, this triple-cream cheese likely originated in Lombardy, where it is widely used today. Some argue it is not a cheese at all, but an acid-coagulated cream.

Maytag blue
blue | cow's milk | US
Invented in Iowa in 1941, this smooth, soft, pungent blue has streaks of spicy blue-gray mold scattered throughout its pale white interior.

Mimolette
hard | cow's milk | France
This round, annatto-colored orange cheese with a rough gray rind resembles a melon when sliced. Younger versions have a fruity Parmesan-like flavor; hazelnut notes develop when the cheese is well aged.

Mont d'Or
semisoft | cow's milk | France
Known for its captivating woodsy, flowery aroma, this small, flavorful cheese has a soft, undulating interior and a thick, pinkish orange rind dusted with white.

Montasio
semifirm, hard | cow's milk | Italy
This lightly pockmarked cheese, made in Friuli–Venezia Giulia, is sold at various stages of maturation, including *fresco* (lightly aged), *mezzano* (semi-aged), or *stagionato* (aged). As it ages, its color shifts from ivory to lightly golden to straw colored, its flavor deepens, and its texture changes from springy to brittle.

Montbriac
soft-ripened | cow's milk | France
Coated with gray ash and splotched with white mold, this rich-tasting cheese from Auvergne is similar to Brie, but is creamier and smaller and has just a touch of blue veining. It is best eaten ripe and oozy.

Monte Enebro
semisoft | goat's milk | Spain
A goat's milk cheese from La Mancha, Monte Enebro is a large, flattened log with white and gray molds covering its rind. Dense and creamy with a hint of juniper (*enebro*), it has a full-bodied flavor that becomes saltier and more pungent with age.

Monterey Jack
semifirm | cow's milk | California
First made in the 1840s, this mild, moist, buttery all-purpose cheese is excellent for melting.

Morbier
semisoft | cow's milk | France
This dense, pale yellow cheese is marked horizontally by a single vein of blue-black vegetable ash to denote milk from two different milkings. It melts well and can be used for gratins and fondues, or as you would raclette.

Mozzarella, fresh
fresh | cow's, water buffalo's milk | Italy
Sweet, earthy, moist, and sliceable, this iconic stretched cheese is a favorite topping for pizza or companion to tomatoes. Its texture should be elastic, but not rubbery.

Mozzarella, low-moisture
semifirm | cow's milk | Italy
A firm, stretchy texture, mild taste, and excellent melting quality make this the preeminent pizza cheese.

Muenster
washed-rind | cow's milk | France
This creamy, pale yellow Alsatian cheese has a pungent smell, an appealing sweet, savory, and yeasty taste, and a snowy white rind. The similarly spelled Munster cheese, which originated in the United States, has a relatively bland, white paste and an orange rind.

Murcia al Vino
semifirm | goat's milk | Spain
Known as "drunken goat" in the United States, this smooth, mildly floral cheese has a purple rind (from bathing in red wine) and an intense white interior.

Neufchâtel

soft-ripened | cow's milk | France

One of Normandy's great cheeses, Neufchâtel has an edible bloomy rind, a rich, creamy, salty flavor, and a grainy texture. It is molded in a variety of shapes, though a heart is the classic form. (Do not confuse this French cheese with the U.S. cheese of the same name, which is a reduced-fat cream cheese.)

Paneer

fresh | cow's, water buffalo's milk | India

This firm, ivory-colored, mild cheese is often used in vegetable dishes (such as with spinach in *saag paneer*).

Parmigiano-Reggiano

hard | cow's milk | Italy

Brittle and crumbly, and with a salty, piquant flavor, Parmiginao-Reggiano (also known as Parmesan) has been made in Emilia-Romagna for at least seven hundred years. To ensure you are getting the real thing, look for the name stenciled vertically on the rind. Although it is best known as a grating cheese, it is also eaten in chunks as part of a cheese course, sometimes with balsamic vinegar or honey.

Pavé d'Affinois

soft-ripened | cow's milk | France

Made in the Lyon region, this soft-ripened cheese is similar to Brie or Camembert, with a fruity flavor and grassy finish. Its name derives from the French word for "cobblestone," which describes its distinctively chunky, squarish profile.

pecorino

hard | sheep's milk | Italy

The word *pecorino* simply indicates that a cheese is made from sheep's milk. Pecorino cheeses come in a variety of regional styles, with grainy, sharp, robust pecorino romano, from the area around Rome, the best known. Pecorino sardo, from Sardinia (Fiore Sardo is the DOC version), is slightly drier and more piquant than its Roman cousin. Pecorino toscano, from Tuscany, which is used as a table cheese when young and grated when aged, tastes of nuts and caramel.

Petit Ardi Gasna

semifirm | sheep's milk | Spain

The rind of this small, cylindrical traditional Basque cheese is rubbed with ground *piment d'Espelette*, a mild red pepper similar to paprika. Its texture is rich and smooth and its flavor nutty.

Piave

hard | cow's milk | Italy

Full bodied and slightly sweet, this straw-colored cheese is primarily used for grating, much in the same way Parmesan is used.

Pont-l'Éveque

washed-rind | cow's milk | France

This well-known square cheese from Normandy has a pale yellow, fine-textured interior. Despite its moldy barnyard odor, it has a sweet flavor with a savory hit.

Port-Salut

semisoft | cow's milk | France

Made in round, thick disks, this smooth and velvety cheese, with its pale yellow interior and orange rind, is admired for its smoky aroma and light acidity.

Provolone

semifirm (stretched-curd) | cow's milk | Italy

A stretched-curd cheese, provolone is available in two styles. *Dolce,* aged for just two or three months, is pale, supple, mild, and smooth and becomes stringy when cooked. *Piccante*, which is typically aged for at least six months, is darker and more strongly flavored, with a hint of spice.

Queso Fresco *see Farmer Cheese*

Queso Iberico

hard | cow's, goat's, sheep's milk | Spain

Similar to Manchego, this cheese is made from a blend of three milks, which yields a balanced, wonderfully complex yet mild flavor. It has a firm texture and is used as both a table cheese and a grating cheese.

Raclette

semisoft | cow's milk | France

With its nutty, sweet flavor, raclette is an excellent melting cheese and an alpine staple. A block of the cheese is traditionally placed near a fire to melt the surface, which is then scraped off the block and spread on bread or boiled potatoes.

Reblochon

washed-rind | cow's milk | France

A soft-ripened cheese from the mountainous Haute-Savoie, Reblochon has a pinkish orange rind, an oozy center, and a yeasty aroma and earthy flavor reminiscent of alpine flowers.

Red Leicester
semifirm | cow's milk | England

This historic farmstead cheese is similar to Cheddar, but it is milder, crumbles more easily, and is both russet red and slightly spicy due to the addition of annatto. Aging can range from three months to one year, with the latter yielding a hard cheese ideal for grating.

Ricotta
fresh | cow's, sheep's milk | Italy

Traditionally made only from whey, rather than from curds like most cheeses, ricotta nowadays often includes skim or whole milk for a richer, creamier product. Factory-produced ricotta is typically grainy; artisanal versions, which are moist and soft, can be a revelation.

Ricotta Salata
semifirm | cow's, sheep's milk | Italy

When fresh ricotta is salted (*salata*), pressed, and dried, this delicious, snow white cheese, ideal for grating, is the result.

Roaring Forties Blue
blue | cow's milk | Australia

King Island, south of Melbourne, puts Australia on the cheese aficionado's map with this award-winning blue. A coating of dark blue wax prevents the growth of a rind and retains moisture, rendering this full-bodied cheese sweet, savory, and creamy.

Robiola
soft-ripened | cow's, goat's, sheep's milk | Italy

Robiola cheese, which is found in Lombardy and Piedmont, varies dramatically, depending on both the milk and the producer. It usually has a soft, supple paste and an earthy flavor. The youngest versions are moist and sweet; aged cheeses are sharper and quite zesty.

Rocamadour
natural-rind | goat's milk | France

This small, nutty, aromatic raw-milk cheese is creamy white with a wrinkled rind.

Romano
hard | cow's, goat's, sheep's milk | Italy

Cheeses made in the area around Rome are called romano. Those made form sheep's milk are called pecorino romano (*see* Pecorino). Tangy caprino romano is made from goat's milk, and mild vacchino romano is made from cow's milk. In general, romanos are similar to Parmesan, but saltier and sharper in flavor.

Roquefort
blue | sheep's milk | France

One of the world's best-known blues, Roquefort is made from rich, creamy sheep's milk cheese and is aged in limestone caves in the rustic and harsh Rouergue region of southern France. It has a buttery texture and a strong, spicy flavor with a hint of burnt sugar.

Saint Agur Blue
blue | cow's milk | France

First made in 1988, Saint Agur is a relative newcomer to the French cheese world. A double cream made from pasteurized cow's milk and cream, it is a decadent, spreadable cheese with green veining that lends mild spice and little saltiness.

Saint-Marcellin
soft-ripened | cow's milk | France

This delectably soft and easy-to-spread bloomy-rind cheese is produced in petite rounds in the Rhône-Alpes region of eastern France, and is sold in a ceramic dish.

Saint-Nectaire
washed-rind | cow's milk | France

The rugged mountainous landscape of the Auvergne is recalled in the earthy aroma of this creamy, soft cheese that evokes cut grass, sweet hay, and wildflowers.

Sbrinz
hard | cow's milk | Switzerland

This hard mountain cheese, made from whole milk in huge wheels, has a gold rind and pale yellow interior. Ideal for grating and shaving in the same manner as Parmesan, its higher butterfat content makes it less salty and smoother than its skim-milk Italian counterpart.

Selles-sur-Cher
natural-rind | goat's milk | France

A Loire Valley classic, this creamy, milky-tasting cheese has a smooth, white, fine-textured paste. A dusting of ash on the exterior encourages the growth of an edible grayish surface mold that protects the delicate interior.

Shropshire Blue
blue | cow's milk | England

Annatto lends an amber hue to this dense-textured blue. Its sharp, spicy, potent flavor recalls a Stilton in disguise. Despite the name, it has no genuine tie to Shropshire. Instead, it was created in Scotland in the 1970s, and is now made in Nottinghamshire.

Sottocenere

semifirm | cow's milk | Italy

Studded with slivers of truffle, rubbed with ash (*sottocenere* means "under ash"), and coated in spices, this smooth-textured, supple cheese delivers a complex and heady flavor.

Stilton

blue | cow's milk | England

Rivaling Roquefort for the blue cheese crown, Stilton is a cylindrical cheese with a creamy, straw-colored interior, an aromatic tang, and a dry, rough brownish rind. Jagged blue lines of mold radiate out from its center.

Taleggio

washed-rind | cow's milk | Italy

Traditionally aged in natural caves, this soft-ripened cheese has a rosy rind, a strong, sweet aroma, and a buttery, fruity flavor that is milder than its smell.

Teleme

semisoft | cow's milk | California

According to legend, this Northern California native with Greek roots is the result of a batch of feta gone deliciously wrong. The cheese has a distinctive pinkish rind and white interior, with a soft texture and pleasantly gamey, tart flavor.

Tête de Moine

semifirm | cow's milk | Switzerland

This cheese has a pale yellow paste, a dry brown rind, and a strong aroma. The name, which translates as "monk's head," hints at the cheese's eight-hundred-year monastic history. One story claims its name derives from its pale interior surrounded by a darker ring, like the shaved tonsure of a monk's head. A special tool called a *girolle* shaves off thin, delicate curls of the cheese that best bring out its flavor.

Tilsiter

semifirm | cow's milk | Switzerland

Also known as Tilsit, this classic Swiss cheese is punctuated with small, irregular holes and covered with a dark yellow rind. It is often flavored with caraway seeds or peppercorns, and pairs well with beer and rye bread. Created by Swiss settlers in Prussia in the nineteenth century, the cheese is named after the city of Tilsit (now Sovetsk, Russia).

Toma Piedmontese

semifirm | cow's milk | Italy

The term *toma* encompasses a group of soft and semifirm Italian cheeses. This *toma* from Piedmont has a long and venerable history. Made from the milk of two consecutive milkings, the paste is buttery and rich in texture. Depending on age, the color ranges from pale yellow to russet red and the flavor from sweet to savory.

Tomme de Savoie

semifirm | cow's milk | France

Made from the skim milk that remains after the cream has been removed for making richer cheese, this smooth cheese has a yellow paste and a dry, powdery rind. Its flavor embraces a medley of subtle tastes: smoke, herbs, flowers, and nuts.

Trou du Cru

washed-rind | cow's milk | France

This soft-ripened cheese, with its yellowish interior and pinkish orange rind, is from one of France's premier winemaking regions, Burgundy's Côte d'Or. During production, the cheese is repeatedly washed in brine, with a final washing in marc (French grappa), which imparts a pungent barnyard aroma and a strong flavor.

Valdeón

blue | cow's, goat's milk | Spain

The mold spores of limestone caves create in this rustic cheese blue-green veins similar to Stilton's, but with a more pungent aroma, saltier bite, and cleaner finish. The cheese is wrapped in sycamore or chestnut leaves.

Wensleydale

semifirm | cow's milk | England

This moist and crumbly cheese is made in five distinct varieties in northern England. Honey notes are balanced with varying degrees of sharpness, depending on variety. Wensleydale sometimes contains cranberries, and is well suited to fruit pairings in general.

Zamorano

hard | sheep's milk | Spain

This ghostly pale cheese with a nearly black rind is rubbed with olive oil throughout the aging process, causing the rind to darken and imparting an exceptionally nutty, rich flavor.

american artisanal cheeses to try

**Achadinha Goat Cheese Company's
Capricious** I Petaluma, CA
Based outside the town of Petaluma, in Northern
California's Sonoma County, Achadinha is home
to sixteen hundred goats. Owners Jim and Donna
Pacheco maintain that natural aging in the fresh
breezes of the Pacific makes the difference in their
goat's milk cheeses. Pressed, aged Capricious, with its
sweet and mild taste, is the breakout star of the line.

Adante Dairy's Legato I Santa Rosa, CA
This semisoft cheese, made from the rich milk of Jersey
cows, follows the traditional recipe for Camembert. It is
ladled into small molds, turned and salted several times,
and left to ripen for at least three weeks, during which it
develops a wonderfully robust flavor.

**Beecher's Handmade Cheese's
Flagship** I Seattle, WA
Located in Seattle's famed Pike Place Market,
Beecher's proves that Vermont isn't the only place to
find good artisanal Cheddar. White, crumbly Flagship, the
company's signature cheese, is aged for at least a year.

**Beehive Cheese Co.'s Barely Buzzed
and SeaHive** I Uintah, UT
The artisanal cheeses of this Utah company showcase
the milk of Jersey cows, who feed on alfalfa grown
in the mineral-rich soil near the Great Salt Lake. The
rind of Barely Buzzed is rubbed with ground coffee
and crushed lavender, which impart caramel and
butterscotch flavors to the interior of the cheese.
Beehive's newest creation, SeaHive, is rubbed with
local honey and with salt from a nearby ancient seabed.

**Berkshire Cheese Makers'
Berkshire Blue** I Great Barrington, MA
A regular award winner at international cheese
competitions, Berkshire Blue is the single cheese
offered by this producer. The raw milk of Jersey
cows is the uncompromising standard, resulting in a
creamy, not-too-salty blue that is aged for sixty days.

**Bellwether Farms'
San Andreas** I Sonoma County, CA
Inspired by the sheep's milk cheeses of Italy, the owners
of this farm became sheep-dairy pioneers in California.
San Andreas is a semifirm, raw-milk cheese made in the
style of a Tuscan pecorino, but with a smoother texture
and a deliciously sour finish.

**Capriole Farmstead Goat Cheeses'
Sofia, Wabash Cannonball, and Piper's
Pyramide** I Greenville, IN
Located in southern Indiana, Capriole was one of
the earliest producers of artisanal goat cheeses in the
United States. Its Sofia, which has a wrinkled, grayish
white rind and a fresh milky flavor, is gently marbled
with edible ash that increases its alluring tang. Ash also
peeks through the bloomy rind of Wabash Cannonball,
a small, spherical soft-ripened cheese with a delicate
texture that becomes denser and more crumbly with
age. Piper's Pyramide, velvety, creamy, and mildly sweet,
with just a hint of mustiness, is sprinkled with paprika
in place of the ash, which is how it came to be named
after the makers' red-haired granddaughter, Piper.

Cato Corner Farm's Hooligan I Colchester, CT
This small Connecticut farm turns out a pungent, soft
and creamy washed-rind cheese lovingly described
as "fabulously stinky." The award-winning Hooligan is
treated to an unusual combination of buttermilk and
salt, which gives it a handsome orange rind and an
unapologetically farmyardy flavor.

**Consider Bardwell Farm's Dorset, Pawlet,
and Manchester** I West Pawlet, VT
Founded in 1864, this well-established cheese
cooperative produces a trio of premier artisanal
cheeses. The cow's milk Dorset is a gloriously
buttery washed-rind cheese, and Pawlet, also made
from cow's milk, is an Italian-inspired toma, pressed
and aged in hefty brown-rind wheels. Manchester
is a rustic, aged raw goat's milk cheese with an
earthy taste and aroma.

Cowgirl Creamery's Mt Tam and Red Hawk ı Point Reyes Station, CA

Cowgirl Creamery, just north of San Francisco, was founded in 1997 by Sue Conley and Peggy Smith, who began their cheese-making operation in an old barn, using organic milk from the neighboring Straus Family Dairy. Today, they have an array of highly regarded cheeses. Two award-winning favorites: Mt Tam is a luscious triple cream, soft-ripened in small but thick rounds. Red Hawk is a washed-rind cow's milk cheese, treated with a brine solution that turns the rind a reddish orange and gives the cheese a full, robust flavor.

Cypress Grove Chevre's Purple Haze ı Arcata, CA

Cheese-maker Mary Keehn began raising goats a quarter of a century ago to provide hard-to-find goat's milk for her children. She soon found herself making fresh goat's milk cheeses in her kitchen. Her popular small, white disks of Purple Haze are flavored with lavender and fennel pollen, which nicely contrast with the acidic tang of the goat's milk. For details on Keehn's famous Humboldt Fog, see page 210.

Hillman Farm's Harvest ı Colrain, MA

This seasonal New England goat dairy produces its award-winning Harvest cheese from its summer milk. Aged for four to six months, the semifirm, natural-rind cheese has a sweet, grassy flavor and a mild bite.

Jasper Hill Farm's Constant Bliss ı Greensboro, VT

Still-warm milk from its herd of Ayrshire cows is ladled into small molds to make Constant Bliss, the pride of this Vermont sustainable farm. The makers loosely adapted a Chaource recipe to create their sweet and milky, soft-ripened cheese. Shaped in small, stout cylinders, just a hint of orange mold glows under the delicate bloomy rind.

Vermont Shepherd Farm's Vermont Shepherd ı Westminster West, VT

The Ilepi Major family ages the farm's rustic Vermont Shepherd cheese in an underground cave for two to six months, turning each wheel every other day. The result is a semifirm sheep's milk cheese with a brown rind and a delicate, rich, smooth flavor redolent of the herbs and clover the sheep graze on throughout the summer.

Meadow Creek Dairy's Grayson ı Galax, VA

Grayson is made in the style of a Taleggio or Livarot, but with an exceptionally rich, mildly pungent, beefy flavor. This small farmstead producer, located in the mountains of southwestern Virginia, attributes both this unique flavor and the cheese's warm yellow interior to the rich, diverse grazing land available to the dairy's Jersey cows.

Mozzarella Company's Deep Ellum Blue and Hoja Santa ı Dallas, TX

Paula Lambert, founder of Mozzarella Company, devises some innovative and uniquely Texan cheeses. Deep Ellum Blue is a semisoft cow's milk with a supple texture and a robust flavor that is neither too sharp nor too salty. The cheese is bathed in mold rather than injected with it, which creates a blue-tinged exterior but no interior veining. The Hoja Santa is a fresh goat cheese wrapped in the velvety, heart-shaped leaves of the local hoja santa plant, which impart tones of mint and sassafras.

Old Chatham Sheepherding Company's Hudson Valley Camembert and Ewe's Blue ı Old Chatham, NY

Sheep dairies are few and far between in the United States, but sheep's milk cheeses are growing in popularity. Old Chatham is the largest sheep dairy in the country, with a herd of East Friesian crossbred ewes grazing on the hills of the Upper Hudson River Valley. The dairy's Hudson Valley Camembert has been praised as the best domestic version to date of the much-imitated European cheese. The Roquefort-style Ewe's Blue is creamy and rich, less salty than Roquefort, with a mellow tang and gorgeous blue-gray veining.

Point Reyes Farmstead Cheese Company's Original Blue ı Point Reyes Station, CA

Made on the farm with milk from their own herd of 250 Holsteins, this wedge-shaped blue cheese from Marin County, California, is creamy, streaked with ocean-blue mold, and has a subtly salty flavor from the sea air.

Redwood Hill Farm's Bucheret ı Sebastopol, CA

The small, family-run Redwood Hill Farm has been producing goat's milk cheeses in California's wine country for more than forty years. An ode to the Loire Valley's Boucheron, the intense, slightly spicy, young Bucheret has a soft, white edible rind and a delightfully creamy powder-white interior.

Rivers Edge Chèvre's Sunset Bay | Logsden, OR
This operation, located in Oregon's Central Coast Range, produces a number of bloomy-rind and washed-rind goat's milk cheeses. Its silky, savory bloomy-rind Sunset Bay is coated in ash and shot through with a vein of smoky Spanish paprika.

Rogue Creamery's Rogue River Blue, Crater Lake Blue, Smokey Blue | Central Point, Oregon
This creamery, which dates back to the Great Depression, regularly garners attention for its innovative and expanding selection of artisanal blues. Rogue River Blue, made in the style of Roquefort, is aged in caves for up to a year and then wrapped in brandy-soaked grape leaves. The most potent cheese in the line is the Crater Lake Blue, and the most unusual is the Smokey Blue, which is cold smoked over hazelnut shells for an inimitable Oregon cheese.

Sally Jackson Cheeses | Oroville, WA
Sally and Roger Jackson raise their own cows, goats, and sheep in eastern Washington and produce unfussy but delicious soft cheeses from their milk. Most of their output is wrapped in chestnut or grape leaves.

Sweet Grass Dairy's Green Hill | Thomasville, GA
Double-cream Green Hill is a Brie-style soft-ripened cheese made from the milk of Jersey cows that graze on the lush grasses of the rolling south-Georgia pastureland that give this family farm its name. The flavor is earthy and gently salted, yet buttery and sweet.

Thistle Hill Farm's Tarentaise | North Pomfret, VT
The Putnam family employs the same cheese-making methods found in the French alps, using copper vats to warm their organic Jersey cow's milk and then naturally aging the cheese for six months. This process yields a classic farmstead cheese with a smooth texture and earthy flavor, in the style of Abondance.

Tumalo Farms' Classico | Bend, OR
A farmstead cheese from the central Oregon countryside, Classico is made from the raw milk of alfalfa-fed goats and then cave-aged for two to three months. The result is a semifirm cheese that tastes sweet and nutty, with a hint of caramel.

Twig Farm's Goat Tomme West Cornwall, VT
Although this modest Vermont cheese operation has a herd of just twenty-five goats, it turns out half a dozen different cheeses with additional milk from neighboring farms. The Goat Tomme is a small drum of raw-milk cheese aged for about eighty days, with a natural rind and a semifirm texture. Its flavor is earthy with a characteristic goat tang.

Uplands Cheese Company's Pleasant Ridge Reserve | Dodgeville, WI
This washed-rind farmstead cheese from Wisconsin, two-time winner of the American Cheese Society's annual competition, is made with the raw milk from cows that graze on fresh grass and herbs. The subtle flavors in the milk, combined with regular baths in brine as the cheese ages, contribute complex layers of fruity, caramelized flavors to the finished cheese.

Vermont Butter & Cheese Creamery's Bijou and Coupole | Websterville, VT
One of the first purveyors of chèvre in Vermont, Vermont Butter & Cheese is now a thriving producer of butter and of fresh and soft-ripened cheeses. Bijou is a soft-ripened goat's milk cheese in the manner of a petite French crottin. Coupole uses the same recipe, but is formed into a striking dome shape. Both are creamy, sweet cheeses; Bijou is the more robust of the two.

Westfield Farm's Classic Blue Log | Hubbardston, MA
This small farm in central Massachusetts has created an award-winning cheese with a unique appearance: the Classic Blue Log is a cylinder of blue chèvre with a creamy white interior free of any veins and an exterior covered with a growth of blue mold.

Willow Hill Farm's Vermont Brebis and Autumn Oak | Milton, VT
This organic farm ages its cow's and sheep's milk cheeses in its own underground cave. Two of its sheep's milk cheeses have received recognition: Autumn Oak is a smooth and creamy natural-rind cheese with a woodsy mushroom flavor. Vermont Brebis is a small, soft-ripened wheel, with olive and mushroom notes and a luscious, runny texture when ripe.

index

weldon**owen**

415 Jackson Street, Suite 200, San Francisco, CA 94111
Telephone: 415 291 0100 Fax: 415 291 8841
www.weldonowen.com

Weldon Owen is a division of

BONNIER

CHEESE OBSESSION

Conceived and produced by Weldon Owen, Inc.
Copyright © 2010 Weldon Owen, Inc. and Williams-Sonoma, Inc.
This book was previously published as Williams-Sonoma Cheese
All rights reserved, including the right of reproduction
in whole or in part in any form.

Printed and bound in China by 1010 Printing
This edition printed in 2012
10 9 8 7 6 5 4 3 2 1

Library of Congress Cataloging-in-Publication
data is available.

ISBN 13: 978-1-61628-498-5
ISBN 10: 1-61628-498-6

ACKNOWLEDGMENTS
Weldon Owen wishes to thank the following people for their generous support in producing this book:
Alison Attenborough, Kimberly Chun, Ken DellaPenta, Julie Nelson, Carrie Neves, Leigh Noe,
Sarah Putman Clegg, Sharon Silva, and Sharron Wood

PHOTOGRAPHY CREDITS
All photographs by Maren Caruso except:
Pages 13 (bottom right) and 88 (top left) by Anna Williams, page 54 (upper left) by Tucker + Hossler